ALL ABOUT Green Budgerigars

by

Roy Stringer
and
Fred Wright

First Published 1992

ISBN 0 9518145 1 6

Typeset in New Century Schoolbook and Printed in Britain by Spottiswoode Ballantyne, Colchester, Essex, England. Published by Roy Stringer Publications, Somerdale Cottage, Station Road, Westbury, Shropshire.

CONTENTS

Acknowledgements

Roy Stringer and Fred Wright gratefully acknowledge the kindness of Eric Peake in offering us the idea for this series of books and for painting the beautiful Light Green Budgerigar on the cover, the great effort put in by Les Lockey, himself a very successful champion breeder, exhibitor and judge of Budgerigars, in travelling around Britain to take photographs of the experts, their birdrooms and - most importantly - their superb Green Budgerigars specifically for this book, Harry Bryan, for delving into his wonderful memory to recall some outstanding Greens from the past, Bryan Byles, Editor of *Cage & Aviary Birds* and Peter Moss, Editor of *Bird keeper* for their support and advice during the book's preparation. Then, of course, there are the experts who answered dozens of questions in our quest to discover what it is that has brought them success at the highest levels with Green Budgerigars; Jim Moffat, Chris and Arthur Snell, Jorge De Pina and John Woods. We thank them all.

FOREWORD

by Eric Peake

For many years I have contemplated writing a series of books, each dealing with different mutations and colours of Budgerigars and featuring the top breeders of each variety. When it became obvious that my painting commitments were pushing this prospect further into the future I was concerned that delay would mean that some of the great names of the Fancy would not be included. This made up my mind. I decided to pass the idea to Roy Stringer and Fred Wright, as I was sure that they would do justice to the concept. I was delighted to be invited to contribute the forewords and paint the covers of the books – of which this is the first in the series. I was asked to base my comments on what I have observed when painting both the "Ideals" for several national societies and specific Budgerigars that have won major honours.

The Light Green is the most numerous and popular member of the group which forms the Normal Greens. My first Budgerigars, back in 1947, were a pair of small Light Greens but it was not until I saw a truly magnificent Light Green exhibited by Tom Rothery that my aspirations turned towards the variety. I purchased a son of this magnificent bird and began a small Light Green stud of my own. Light Greens have made tremendous progress in substance over the last few years but, in the process, have suffered in the area of colour. One does not often see the crisp yellow and grey wing coloration that was common years ago. Too much green is displayed on the head, back and wings, where the colour should be yellow; the result of crossing normal Light Greens with Opalines. Height above the eye and general skull formation (particularly "frontal") have deteriorated, but size has truly progressed.

Three shades of Normal Greens exist; light (Light Green), medium (Dark Green) and dark (Olive). It is not only in body colour that these differ. There is also a gradation of colour to be seen in the cheeks patches, tails and primary flights of the wings. Dark Greens and Olives are very uncommon in today's exhibition Budgerigar Fancy which is a great pity as they are lovely Budgerigars and the Fancy as a whole could only benefit from more of them being bred. The pairings most likely to propagate good Dark Greens are Dark Green × Dark Green, Dark Green × Light Green and Olive × Light Green. The first pairing, while also producing Light Greens, is the best mating for breeding Olives. The beauty of the Normal Greens could be under threat unless great care is taken with head markings. If the zebra markings appear forward of the eye they destroy the clarity of the head and with it an essential aspect of the beauty of Light Greens, Dark Greens and Olives. Read on to discover what the top breeders of Normal Greens have to say. I believe you will find it an enjoyable and rewarding experience.

INTRODUCING THE GREENS

The history of Light Greens is the history of Budgerigars. The wild Budgerigar is a Light Green and how long it has been in existence is impossible to tell. However, the Budgerigar was first described by Shaw, the naturalist, in 1794. Then the explorer, John Gould, transported the first living pair from the Liverpool Plain of Southern Australia, where he caught them, to England in 1840. They were bred in captivity soon after. The attractive appearance and lively character of the Budgerigar raised its popularity to amazing heights. According to the early writer on Budgerigars, Dr Karl Russ, between February 1878 and January 1879 almost 190,000 Budgerigars were shipped to Europe by one London importer alone! The Australian government prohibited the exporting of native birds in the 1890s but the free-breeding nature of Budgerigars meant that there were still plenty available. Dr Russ estimated that, in the early 20th century, around 30,000 Budgerigars a year were being bred in Europe. Big stock farms were set up in Germany to export thousands to the USA and Russia.

Light Greens were bred in captivity for more than 30 years before the first colour change (the Light Yellow) was seen but it was in 1915 that a great breakthrough occurred - the breeding of the Dark Green - in the aviaries of the Blanchard Brothers, in Toulouse, France. This event had far greater repercussions than could have been foreseen at the time. It was the creation of the "dark factor" which made this mutation so important. The Dark Green has one dark factor and by merely pairing two Dark Greens together (without the need for a further mutation) a Green Budgerigar with two dark factors was produced in 1916; the variety which we now call the Olive. The Skyblue had already made an appearance around 1880 and combining the dark factor with this brought us the Cobalt (one dark factor) and the Mauve (two dark factors) in the early 1920s. Taylor & Warner's standard work, *Genetic for Budgerigar Breeders* is invaluable reading for anyone who wants to go further into how the colour effects of the various varieties of Budgerigars are produced, but a brief description of what constitutes the dark factor is offered here for those who wish to gain a rudimentary understanding of the mechanics of the creation of body colour.

A Budgerigar's feathers has barbs which carry the elements necessary to display its colour. At the centre of the barb are melanin granules, surrounded by a cloudy layer. Outside that is the cortex which, in Green series Budgerigars contains a yellow pigment. The depth of apparent colour is governed by the density of the pigment, the shape of a section through the barb and the thickness of the cloudy zone. The dark factor was created when a Budgerigar was bred with slimmer-than-usual barbs and a thinner cloudy zone. The same amount of melanin pigment, at the centre of the feather barb, therefore absorbed more light and made the bird look darker. Pairing dark factor birds together produced a Budgerigar with two dark factors with even slimmer barbs and an even thinner cloudy zone. Every Budgerigar variety known has three levels of darkness, whether it is immediately apparent to the human eye or not.

We know all that now, with the benefit of hindsight, but there was much understandable confusion among early breeders of Dark Greens. At first it did not seem to be recognised as a distinct, new mutation. Some were of the opinion that Dark Greens were the result of pairing Yellows with Skyblues – possibly because young Dark Greens often display blue coloration in the lower part of the body plumage. Others felt that Dark Greens and Olives had come from using badly-coloured Yellows – possibly because of the drab coloration of the latter.

Although we can thank the early breeders of Budgerigars for establishing so many varieties and improving them (in exhibition terms) beyond recognition they have much to answer for in their choice of terminology when it comes to the dark factor. The reasons for confusion will be seen in the following explanation of terminology.

The Light Green has no dark factor and is the light shade of the Greens. The Dark Green has one dark factor and is the medium shade of the Greens. The Olive has two dark factors and is the dark shade of the Greens.

For all their beauty, the Dark Green and the Olive never reached the heights of popularity of the Light Green. Indeed, in most serious Budgerigar breeders' studs the Dark Green is a by-product of Light Green breeding and Olives are, for all practical purposes, non-existent. This situation is borne out by the answers and the amount of space taken up by the four experts when dealing with the different Green shades in this book. The arrival of the Grey Green sounded the virtual death-knell of the Olive. Of similar coloration, the newcomer was so much easier to breed to exhibition standards. There was also, perhaps, the creation of false expectation. Pretty paintings of deep green Budgerigars are hardly the ideal preparation for seeing your first Olive which, if a poor example, will be patchy and mud-coloured. The artist's interpretation could well be more descriptive of the Violet Dark Green; more richly coloured but often mistaken for an Olive.

For many years, Light Greens were so superior in all respects that they were used to improve every new variety as it came along. Dr Russ made much of the fact that the further a new colour varied from the Light Green the smaller and weaker it tended to be. Experts, like William Watmough, were for ever recommending crossing other varieties back into Light Greens to prevent them from deteriorating. His phrase "dipping into the Green" has conditioned many a Budgerigar breeder who was brought up with his book, *The Cult of the Budgerigar*, as their bible. The consequence was that the Light Green itself was pulled down in quality and, right up to the present, it is almost impossible to find a "pure" Light Green cock; one that is not carrying hidden factors like Opaline, Cinnamon or Blue. Perhaps the only benefit the Light Green derived from all this outcrossing has been that it helped to maintain its fertility.

At the beginning, the Budgerigar classes at shows were dominated almost entirely by Light Greens. Then their strongest competition came from Light Yellows and Greywings. As new varieties have strengthened, both physically and in their following, the Yellows and Greywings have fallen by the wayside. At the average show, if there are any exhibited at all they can be counted on the fingers of one hand. The Light Green, although it has had its ups and downs, is still at the top and going strong. It regularly provides the winner of major trophies at large shows all over the world including twice best in show at the Budgerigar Society Club Show during the 1980s. The first with a hen bred by C & A Snell and the second a cock bred by John Woods, both among the experts who reveal their methods in this book. At the most recent BS Club Show, in 1991, there were 369 Normal Greens entered which just kept the variety ahead of all the others to be highest entry in the show.

The objective of the authors* of this book – and the other books in the *All about ...* series – is to offer a platform for some of the world's most successful breeders of particular Budgerigar varieties to reveal their techniques, methods, likes, dislikes and hopes for the future. We believe we have succeeded. You will not find the colour standard or scale of points of any organisation for more than one reason. Different countries have different standards. There is a distinct possibility that an international standard could be agreed before the end of the century. If you want to read a particular club's standards you can join the club – the space in this book is better devoted to the opinions of breeders who have proved their ability by winning with Greens at the very highest levels. Colour standards and points allocations vary, but an outstanding Budgerigar is recognised the world over – and as long as there are Budgerigars there will be Light Greens.

**(Roy Stringer, formerly a car designer, is Features Editor of CAGE & AVIARY BIRDS and Fred Wright, by training a technology teacher, is a regular contributor of articles to the same weekly journal. Both are successful champion breeders and exhibitors of Budgerigars and international judges.)*

Harry Bryan looks back

■ *Harry Bryan is the most successful Budgerigar fancier the world has ever known. He began keeping Budgerigars in 1916 and, in 1992, is still enjoying success on the show bench. In the intervening years he saw all of the top Budgerigars in the UK which until recently, in Budgerigar terms, meant the world. His memory is as keen as ever and here he recalls names from the past and a few from the present; the top breeders of Green Budgerigars of their time.*

During the 1930s and 1940s there were, in my opinion, only three fanciers who had top quality Green Budgerigars in depth. They were Ronnie Knight of Leicester, Frank Wardle of Macclesfield and, without boasting, myself. All the top Green awards were taken by us three. Ronnie would take the prize one week, Frank would win the next show and I would step in to take the trophy on the third weekend. Frank and Ronnie went into partnership; an arrangement that lasted about 10 years. Frank Wardle had a super Green cock which won and won and won. It was fitted with a mauve split ring and judges used to look for this. I could not beat it until I put a similar mauve ring on my best Green. Then I started to win! When I was at the top – in the Sutton Coldfield days – I always put down 10 pairs of Greens to breed. From these I would produce around 120 youngsters which would give me around 25 good ones to exhibit.

Several other names come to mind as deserving a mention for the quality of their Green Budgerigars. Alan Elsdon of Macclesfield had some good ones in the 1950s which originated from Frank Wardle's stock. Jim Moffat's father had some good ones and, of course, Jim, himself, has been a powerful Light Green specialist for the past 35 years. Tom Rothery. from Lancashire, was a good fancier who bred excellent Greens for a few years but he never seemed to take many best in show awards with them. Another breeder who has had good Light Greens, without quite dominating with the variety, is my old friend Bill Bancroft. Lance Bradley of Leicester did well for a while. His Greens originated from Fred Watson whose Greens, in turn, came from Doughty & Gripps. When that partnership finished Lance bought their birds and crossed them with Watson stock and did very well. My good friend P.S.W. (Percy) Smith had lots of Greens and enjoyed a fair amount of success. However his strength tended to be in numbers and he did not make as much impact as others at the very highest levels. Maurice Finey had a wonderful stud of Greens in the early 1960s. He bought a Blue cock from me and paired it with an Opaline Light Green hen. That was the start of his Greens. His strength lay in the number of Greens he bred; at least 200 every year. He also won well with one or two Dark Greens. The late Jack Fisher produced several Greens of the very highest quality during the late 1960s and early 1970s. Unfortunately his death robbed the Fancy of a star breeder. More recently the father and son partnership of Arthur and Chris Snell have made an impact on the show bench with their Greens, particularly with hens.

I cannot recall anybody who specialised in Dark Greens or Olives, though Alf Ormerod's name comes to mind when Dark Greens are mentioned. He exhibited a wonderful specimen at the 4th Budgerigar Society Convention, around 1960, and in partnership with Doug Sadler took best in show at the BS Club Show two years running with another outstanding Dark Green. For all that, there has never been a stud which had Dark Greens of quality, in depth.

In the early days Greens were much better coloured than they are today. As each new mutation and combination came along Light Greens particularly were used to improve them - and there were lots in the 1930s including Cinnamons, Fallows, Recessive Pieds, Lutinos, Albinos, Opalines, Greys, Clearwings and Dominant Dutch Pieds. In the process it was the quality of the Greens themselves that suffered. I am sorry to say that the "grass greens" of yesterday seem to have gone for ever.

("The Budgerigar Man", the Harry Bryan story and way of breeding exhibition Budgerigars is available from the publishers of this book)

MEET THE EXPERTS

JIM MOFFAT lives in a small village on the Clyde coast of Scotland, 30 miles from Glasgow. He began keeping Budgerigars in the 1930s and his farsighted father bought him a life-membership of the Budgerigar Society in 1937. Mention the name Moffat, in connection with Budgerigars, and the variety Light Green immediately leaps to mind. When his interest in Budgerigars became serious, Light Greens were the most popular, most competitive and, hence, the most challenging variety. Besides that, Jim Moffat just likes Light Greens. He is not the sort of man who keeps lists of his wins, but he did win the champion Light Green class at the National Exhibition of Cage & Aviary Birds in 1956 and 1957; a time when this class was more difficult to win than any other in the whole show season. He has taken the best in show award at the Scottish Budgerigar Society championship show, with Light Greens on numerous occasions and has taken the Normal Green challenge certificate at the BS Club Show many times. In 1976 his young Light Green cock took the most coveted trophy of all – that for best breeder in show at the BS Club Show and just a year later his hen took the best opposite sex in show award at the same prestigious event. In recent years, business commitments caused his virtual retirement from exhibiting but evidence that his standards never faltered came when he entered and won the champion any age Light Green cock class at the 1991 BS Club Show.

CHRIS AND ARTHUR SNELL form a son and father partnership. They live a little distance apart on South Humberside, in the east of England and manage their own birdrooms. Chris started keeping Budgerigars, with a collection of mixed colours, in 1965 and was soon joined by his father. Two years later they took the best in show award at Grimsby CBS with a young Light Green hen. That was the first step on the road to success. At the BS Club Show that year they saw Class number 1, champion any age Light Green cocks and were in no doubt that this was the colour for them. In 1967 they visited the late Jack Fisher and were very impressed by his Budgerigars – particularly his Greens. The same year Tom Rothery took best in show at Cleethorpes with one of his famous Greens and, after being approached, sent them a Green. That was the first brick in the foundation of what was to become a world-famous stud of Light Greens. Between 1967 and 1991, C.& A. Snell benched more than 50 best in show winners and the same number of best breeders in show; often with hens. The Budgerigar Society Club Show has always been a rewarding show for the Snells: Breeder challenge certificate with a Dark Green cock in 1983, any age CC in 1987 with a Light Green cock and again with a Light Green hen in 1990 and best opposite sex in show with a Light Green hen in 1991. Their greatest triumph at the BS Club Show came in 1984 when their young Light Green hen progressed from winning her class, through taking the CC and best breeder in show, to go on and take the supreme award; best in show.

JORGE LUIS DE PINA is South America's top Budgerigar fancier; a full-time, professional breeder employing two servants in his birdroom. He is sponsored by Trill. They pay for all his seed, stationery and some of his personal expenses. He appears in their TV commercials, has the Trill logo on every nest-box and displayed around his birdroom. He comes from Barra da Tijuca in Brazil, a third-world country with inflation rates of 30 to 40 per cent per month. He has to work hard with his Budgerigars to keep ahead and to make a living. He began keeping Budgerigars in 1965 and since 1979 has visited the UK every year to purchase Budgerigars; retaining some for his own use and selling the rest to other South American fanciers. It is said that he knows the British Budgerigar Fancy better than many who are based in the UK. He had already built up a stud of excellent quality by 1987, when he set out to build the largest and best stud of Light Greens in the world. He keeps many other varieties, such as Violets, Lutinos, and Pieds but his major concern is with his Light Greens. Brazil's biggest Budgerigar show is the "ACPA". Jorge De Pina has taken best in show at this event four times. Budgerigar World, Brazil show has been staged three times and he has taken the best in show and best breeder trophies every time and the best opposite sex awards twice - every time with Light Greens. The largest all-variety show is the Brazilian Championships. On two occasions Jorge's Budgerigars have beaten all of the other types of birds to take the supreme trophy; with a Light Green in 1985 and a Dark Green in 1987.

JOHN WOODS lives at Poulton-le-Fylde, Blackpool in England. He began keeping Budgerigars when only 12 years old but gave up when he was called into the armed forces for National Service. Within a matter of weeks of restarting in 1964 he visited several championship shows in the county of Lancashire. There were two outstanding breeders of Light Green Budgerigars in that area at the time; Tom Rothery of Blackpool and Jimmy Kenyon of Clitheroe. Both frequently took major awards at the top shows. Visits to Mr Kenyon did not result in the acquisition of birds. His stud was small and there was a waiting list for his surplus stock. Tom Rothery's stud was most impressive and John managed to buy a few Budgerigars from him over a period of time. However, Rothery Greens were in great demand and he had to be satisfied with Skyblues and Greys. As the stud developed, John gained successes with Light Greens at championship shows. Among the more notable of these was taking awards such as best in show, best breeder and best opposite sex awards at shows as prestigious as Lancashire, Cheshire & North Wales BS area championship, the Great Norwestern, Preston, Bury and Liverpool. However, without doubt, John Woods' greatest achievement was taking the best-in-show award at the 1988 Budgerigar Society Club Show with an outstanding Light Green cock. Since then he has curtailed his exhibiting somewhat while he has been reorganising the balance of his stud.

CHAPTER 1

THEIR BIRDROOMS

Describe your birdroom.

Jim Moffat:

My birdroom is a timber structure and measures 30ft by 20ft (9.1m × 6.1m). It is very old-fashioned and has been moved five times. It would have made more sense to build a new brick birdroom when we moved to our present house 30 years ago. A brick structure would be more attractive and require less maintenance. Having retained the old one – just out of sentiment – at the time of writing I have an architect working on the design of a brick birdroom. The floor of my existing birdroom is solid and the sloping roof is equipped with sliding windows which greatly add to the natural ventilation. The internal flight is large at 24ft by 12ft (7.3m × 3.6m) and it also has large sliding windows which are opened in summer. Young birds develop well with so much room to exercise and their parents are moved into the flight when the breeding season is over. The cocks are returned to stock cages in October. I discontinued the use of outside flights when cats became a nuisance and because I suffered unaccountable losses of young birds. The view from my birdroom is beautiful, over the sea to the Isle of Arran, but the associated winds made outside flights unusable at some times of the year. The winds do not seem to disturb the birds within the room. The internal layout is quite traditional with cages on two of the walls. There are 48 breeding cages in all, measuring 3ft × 3ft × 2ft (91cm × 91cm × 61cm). The removal of dividing slides makes them into long flight cages when the breeding season is over. At one time I used external nest-boxes but my aviary attendant of the time became very proficient at knocking them with his head as he went around the birdroom. This disturbed me – and the birds – so I reverted to the internal desk-type nest-box with its entrance hole in the top. They measure 8in × 6in × 6in (20cm × 15cm × 15cm), are equipped with a concave, and are positioned on the breeding cage floors. When the pairs are put together I half-fill each nest-box with sawdust. Internal nest-boxes take longer to inspect, but I still prefer them. The equipment, which is as conventional as the layout, consists of electric lighting, thermostatically-controlled electric heaters, ionisers, mains water and a water heater. Some of the automatic watering systems I have seen in other breeders' birdrooms looked rather unhygienic to me.

Jim Moffat's birdroom has been moved five times, being placed in its present location in 1962. Since this photograph was taken the outside flight has been dispensed with and the interior (below) has been arranged to create the maximum possible flying space.

Chris and Arthur Snell:

Chris's birdroom is brick-built and measures 35ft × 15ft × 8ft (10.7m × 4.6m × 2.4m) high. The wooden floor is set on low walls. The room's walls are lined with "Laconite" plastic-faced hardboard. Two 8ft × 4ft (2.4m × 1.2m) windows face south west. Two 15ft × 6ft (4.6m × 1.8m) inside flights connect to large, L-shaped outside flights. Being outside in the sun and rain strengthens Budgerigars and flying relatively long distances – with a right-angle turn in the middle builds up muscles. Any birds that do not do well in large flights are moved to Arthur's establishment. The back wall of the room accommodates four tiers of cages. Each tier contains 12 cages which each measures 30in wide × 20in high × 24in deep (76cm × 51cm × 61cm). Four stock cages bring the total to 52. Outside-mounted nest boxes, constructed from ⅜in (9mm) plywood, measure 10½ in long × 9in wide × 6½ in deep (27cm × 23cm × 17cm). As well as 2in (5cm) thick concaves, the boxes are fitted with internal landing blocks to prevent hens stepping straight onto the eggs. Small internal boxes are provided for chicks when they leave the nest. There are storage units for seed and equipment. Fluorescent lighting is controlled by a timer but nightlights are left on all of the time. Heating is by thermostatically-governed electric convector heaters. Ionisers have been found to keep the air cleaner and Vapona strips keep down moths, flies and mites. Both birdrooms have ornamental ponds outside to increase the humidity within.

Arthur has two birdrooms. The first is of timber construction, clad with plastic weather board, insulated with fibre glass, and measures 16ft × 8ft × 8ft (4.9m × 2.4m × 2.4m). It contains 16 cages (each 30in × 24in × 21in (76cm × 61cm × 53cm)) with removable trays and a 12ft × 8ft (3.6m × 2.4m) inside flight which connects to an outside flight. An extractor fan and air vents keep the atmosphere fresh. The second room is brick built and measures 9ft 6in × 9ft 6in × 7ft (2.9m × 2.9m × 2.1m). This contains breeding cages and a 15ft × 7ft (4.6m × 2.1m) inside flight which leads to an outside flight of the same proportions. Nest-boxes, lighting and heating arrangements are the same as Chris's. Thermostats are set to maintain the temperature at 50deg F (10deg C). Water is not laid on in any of the Snell birdrooms, neither are there sink units, as neither's marital partner objects to the kitchen being used to wash feeders and drinkers.

Jorge De Pina:

I have two birdrooms. The main one is 98ft × 16ft (30m × 5m) and is completely equipped with flights, cages and all the necessary equipment. The second, my quarantine room, measures 16ft × 5ft (5m × 1.5m) and is equipped with cages and a sink. The main room is brick-built and has a sloping roof of clay tiles set on wooden battens. There are windows along the front that open and can be covered by plastic frames. There are five inside

Chris Snell's 35ft (10.7m) long, brick-built birdroom is very well proportioned and its appearance is further improved by its wrap-round outside flights. Equally well-planned are the 48 breeding cages (below) which are accommodated on the back wall.

Jorge De Pina's main birdroom is 98ft (30m) long and is equipped with five inside and three outside flights. The 150 breeding cages it houses are of all-wire construction.

flights two measuring 13ft × 6ft 6in (4m × 2m) and the others 8ft 2in × 3ft 3in (2.5m × 1m), 16ft × 6ft 6in (5m × 2m) and 6ft 6in × 3ft 3in (2m × 1m). Three outside flights connect to the internal ones. The larger ones (13ft × 13ft (4m × 4m)) house adults and youngsters over 6 months of age. The smaller flight (6ft 6in × 3ft 3in (2m × 1m)) houses young birds between 10 weeks and 6 months. The room is fitted with 150 breeding cages; 107 of them on the back wall. External, wooden nest boxes measure 12½in × 7in × 7in (32cm × 18cm x18cm) and are equipped with a novel, half-height divider which effectively provides them with two compartments. An extractor fan and a water spray set above the roof reduce the temperature within the room in hot weather. The latter also helps to maintain humidity. There are two sinks with hot and cold water and mains drainage. An electrically operated brush facilitates the washing of drinkers. A humidifier helps to control the internal environment. No heating is required in Brazil because of the climate and no automatic watering system is needed because labour is cheap. However, there IS a need for a refrigerator and a freezer.

John Woods:

My birdroom is 36ft long by 12ft wide (10.9m × 3.6m) and is constructed from 3in × 2in (7.6cm × 5cm) framing clad with sheets of thick external plywood. It has a timber floor and is set on concrete blocks which raise it 18in (46cm) above a bed of concrete at ground level. It has a slightly sloping flat roof. The interior is lined with plastic coated board and the cavity is filled with fibreglass insulation. This keeps the room warm in winter and cool in summer. In the roof are two 5ft × 4ft (1.5m × 1.2m) domed skylights. The only other windows are three which measure 2ft × 2ft (61cm × 61cm) in the front wall. Ventilation is provided by four plastic air vents at floor level and another four set high in the walls. These alone provide sufficient ventilation when my stock is at minimum level but as the number of birds increases through the breeding season a large extractor fan is employed. The birdroom is entered via a safety porch, through a door in the front wall, 6ft (1.8m) from the left hand end. Inside, on the left is a 5ft 6in (1.7m) wide flight which runs the full 12ft (3.6m) width of the room. On the right is a sink and storage units and beyond these are two 11ft × 6ft (3.3m × 1.8m) inside flights. Each connects, through adjustable bob-holes, or one of the windows, to 12ft × 12ft (3.6m × 3.6m) outside flights. I like large flights as they improve the quality of Budgerigars' lives and keeps them healthy. The other walls of the room accommodate 54 breeding cages; each measuring 30in × 16in × 16in (76cm × 41cm × 41cm) made from plywood and painted white. The edges of cages and dividers are covered by metal strips to protect them from being gnawed. In consequence, they are as good now as when they were made 15 years ago. Each cage front has a small door at the top right-hand side which, when opened, gives access into an externally mounted nest-box. The boxes are 9½ in long × 6½ in wide × 9in high (24cm × 16cm × 23cm). They lie along the cage front. A 4½ (11cm) inspection door opens at

John Woods' 36ft (10.9m) long birdroom is well screened by shrubs. The interior (below) is arranged on classic lines with flights on one side and breeding cages on the other side of a wide passageway.

Budgerigars are very adaptable and will breed in a variety of cages. In Scotland, Jim Moffat uses traditional tiers of wooden cages while in the hotter climate of Brazil, Jorge De Pina chooses all-wire cages.

the concave end so that the hen can retreat calmly into the cage, through the access hole, by way of a stepping block. The extractor fan, internal and external lighting are all controlled by timers. The sink unit has a cold water supply, heated when required by an electric flash heater. I also use an ioniser to keep the air fresh. The room is so well insulated that there is no need for fixed heaters. I bring in a portable electric heater when necessary; for about four weeks each year. Lighting is by fluorescent tubes which run the full length of the room alternating, "warm-glo" and "violet" hues. I leave the lights on all day but I believe that the number of hours of light is only a small part of the solution to infertility. I consider that intensity of light plays a large part in stimulating Budgerigars to breed. As the timer switches off the main lighting it switches on two 15 watt red "pigmy" bulbs which act as nightlights. These provide enough illumination to permit a hen to return to her nest if she leaves it because she has been disturbed.

CHAPTER 2

MANAGEMENT

Describe a typical day's activity in your birdroom during the breeding season.

Jim Moffat:

I still enjoy the luxury of an aviary attendant who looks after cleaning, watering and feeding. I attend to pairing, nest-box inspections, softfood requirements and general supervision. On a normal day during the breeding season I spend about an hour each morning, and about the same in the evening, in the birdroom. I check the nest-boxes at about 7 o'clock in the morning and sometimes for a second time in the evening. I disturb eggs as

Although he still enjoys the luxury of an aviary attendant, Jim Moffat still gets a lot of pleasure from undertaking nest-box inspections himself. He uses interior, desk-type boxes which are lifted from the cage to be examined.

little as possible. There is no need to lift an egg to see if it is fertile. Even without using an inspection torch it becomes obvious after a few days that an egg is full. As the time for hatching approaches I am always on the look-out for the flash of red that tells me that a chick has emerged from the shell. I always think: "Red is for go!" Fostering eggs and chicks to balance the sizes of nests ("Cabinet reshuffles" I call them) takes place at week-ends. Other than ringing, I try not to interfere with chicks. At weekends I spend considerably more time with my birds, observing the pairs that are not making progress and trying to discover what the problem is. I find one of the greatest dilemmas is deciding just how patient to be with hens that are not laying. So often, a pair of which you have great hopes lets you down. When a hen fails to go to nest I try to be patient and wait another week before splitting the pair. Then I may see the pair mating and decide to delay yet another week. The temptation is to leave a pair for longer than I should, but – as in life – without hope there is nothing.

Chris and Arthur Snell:

Although we manage our two halves of the stud in the same way, the fact that Chris works full time and Arthur is retired means that there is some difference in the timing. As Chris's routine is the more tightly timed, that is the one we will record. I check at 7.30am to make sure there are no sick birds, which takes no more than five minutes. In the evening, on returning from work I take a quick look around before taking my evening meal and preparing the softfood. I return to the birdroom at around 7.00pm, when I work from cage to cage inspecting nest-boxes and feeding. Seed dishes have husks removed and are topped up. Every two weeks the dishes are completely emptied (any seed goes to the flights) and refilled. Records are made directly into the register. I do not use cards. If there are other demands on my time I can deal with 48 pairs in one hour. Drinking water is changed every third day. When I have more time it is changed more often. I usually leave the birdroom around 10.00pm, though I do stay longer sometimes. At weekends I follow the same routine with the added tasks of removing large droppings, topping up grit pots, replacing cuttlefish bone, changing concaves and renewing sawdust in nest-boxes. Cleaning is a constant operation and so there is no big clean up required.

Jorge De Pina:

All the general management in my birdroom is carried out by my servants, but I carefully supervise all of their work. They work to a plan set at the start of the week. Because the Budgerigars are a full-time business there is no set day for a major clean up, it goes on all the time. The first job of the day, which starts around 8.00am is to clean the drinkers

Nest-boxes come in all shapes and sizes. This type, used by Jorge De Pina, has a novel interior division which prevents eggs from being scattered and permits older chicks to nestle away from their mother.

Accurate record keeping is essential if Budgerigars' pedigrees are to have any value. Here, Jorge De Pina makes notes about a young Light Green.

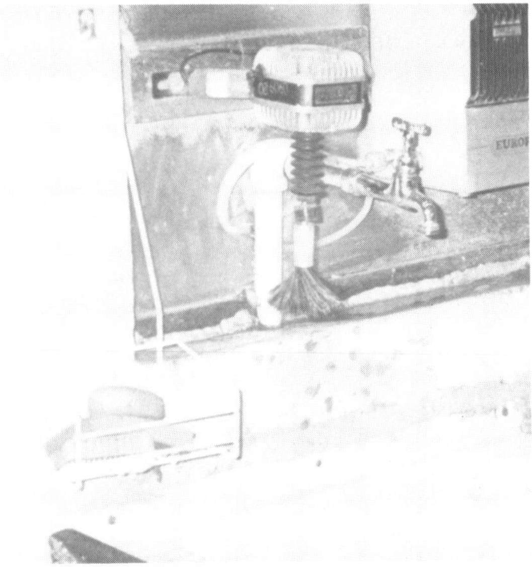

The first job of the day, in the De Pina birdroom, is cleaning drinkers using this motor-driven brush.

thoroughly. I have a small electric motor fitted with a brush, positioned over the sink. The tube of the drinkers fit onto the brush and cleaning is made very easy. The bottoms of the drinkers are cleaned in the same way, but a small brush is sometimes required to clean out awkward corners. All drinking water is changed every morning; the first job. It is very warm in Brazil and I believe it is important for my Budgerigars to have fresh water. The next job is to prepare the softfood. This is made fresh each day in a liquidiser. It is fed to the birds while it is still absolutely fresh and only in amounts that can be consumed quickly. The amount consumed by each pair is monitored every day and the measure offered the following day is adjusted accordingly. If softfood was left uneaten it would soon become stale and I do not wish my birds to eat anything other than fresh food. The softfood dishes are removed around 6.00pm to be washed ready for the next morning. Seed is fed in plastic hoppers; much smaller versions of those used for poultry. The seed level is checked three times a week and the husks are blown off. It is not only breeding pairs that are kept in cages. All young birds are caged until they are well into their first moult. As potential show birds come through the moult they also are caged. There is a fair amount of segregation. Show birds are kept in the colour groups and young stock is kept separate from over-year birds. Overall, a far greater proportion of my stock is kept in cages than that of most other breeders and this causes a lot more work than if they were mainly housed in flights. Even so, I believe that the results - both in breeding and showing - prove that the birds benefit from the way that I house them. Although there is no strict programme of when the extra jobs are undertaken, I like to have the birdroom in its best condition by the week-end. Friday is always the busiest day. The cages and the flights will have been cleaned through the week, so on Friday the refrigerator and the windows are cleaned. When there are as many Budgerigars in a birdroom as I keep, the job is never done. Cleaning, like maintenance, is a continuous process.

John Woods:

If a fancier is keeping a substantial number of birds he needs to be well organised and make the most of his time. I have established daily and weekly routines which have now become so much of a habit that I can carry them out without having to think what to do next. My bird day during the breeding season always starts by loading and arranging my trolley. This is 4ft (1.2m) high and has three plastic shelves set within a metal frame. It is mounted on casters which means that it can be moved easily around the birdroom. On the trolley I place a large jug of seed, a dish of bread and milk, a dish of soft egg food, a box containing fine wood chippings, clean seed dishes, grit, grit pots, fresh cuttlefish bone and closed rings. Starting at the far end of the birdroom I replenish the food in each cage and attend to its nest-box. The nest-box has its own ritual. If there are only eggs these are lifted carefully, marked with care and returned to the same position without having been rotated at all. If there are youngsters, these are removed and placed into the box containing wood chippings. Any eggs still in the box, waiting to hatch can then be examined and any cleaning of the box carried out. Having done that, I check the rings on the youngsters, clean off any dirt and rotate the ring on the leg to ensure that there is no build up of excreta or woodchips inside the ring which might cut off the blood supply to the foot which could, at worst, result in the loss of the foot. When the cages are completed, I refill the water pots. After that I feed the birds in the flights and follow on with the daily clean up. With Budgerigars, as with all livestock, there are always unforseen daily happenings which have to be taken care of. The weekly jobs, such as cleaning the flights and washing the water pots are shared out through the week rather than leaving them all until the same day.

Describe the activities in you birdroom during the lead up to a show.

Jim Moffat:

Since I only exhibit my Budgerigars about once a year I do not have to concern myself with keeping birds in show condition for several weeks. Even so, I believe that exhibiting so infrequently has its disadvantages. You have a much greater chance of scoring big successes if you exhibit at numerous events throughout the show season. To do well on the show bench you need to devote a lot of time to your birds; more time than I have been able to give having been Chairman and Managing Director of a company that employs 2,500 people for many years. Though I must admit that showing infrequently also suits my temperament. At weekends I run any promising birds through the show cages, as much for my own pleasure as anything else. A Budgerigar that relaxes and whistles when it is in a show cage improves its chances greatly when it gets to a show. I select my best prospects about six weeks in advance of the show and house them, 12 to a stock cage. The selected birds are made more familiar with the show cage and their tails and flights are inspected. Here is a dilemma. There is no point in exhibiting Budgerigars with broken tails but there are occasions when they never grow again after being pulled. On balance, I remove broken flights and tails - very carefully. The potential show team is sprayed with cold water, heavily at first and becoming lighter as the show approaches.

During the week prior to the show one obviously prepares and labels the show cages - making sure that the entries are correct. However, my principle activity and concern is the task of despotting. Due to a combination of poor eyesight and nervousness I am not as proficient at this important task as I used to be. With my very limited exhibiting programme, just one slip could mean that my best bird would miss a whole show season.

Chris and Arthur Snell:

The show team is sprayed, with plain water, every second day. In summer I spray them at 6.00pm, as soon as I get in from work. In winter I spray in the mornings before going to work. Spraying is done in an old show cage with holes drilled in its bottom to permit water to drain away. Our stock cages are kept clean and so our show birds do not get very dirty and, because they are never overcrowded we do not get many broken flights. We have no revolvers or swings in the flights and this also means less broken feathers. If a bird DOES break a feather what we do about it depends upon its feather texture. If it is fine-feathered (a Yellow) we remove it. If it is coarse-feathered (a Buff) we leave it well alone. Those birds which need a little extra weight are fed soaked oats every day. Any bird that begins to lose show condition is returned immediately to the flights. We never try to hold it back in order to show it as being exhibited when it is not fully fit takes too much out of a bird.

The cages containing the show team are cleaned every other day; a very important measure. From the Tuesday before the show, tweezers and a toothbrush are use to tease pin feathers into opening. Any sign of bleeding (feather quills, flights, claws) is stopped by dabbing with tincture of iodine. Bloodstains are removed by washing with neat *Vanodine V18* on cotton wool, and then rinsed with clean water. The feathers MUST be wet before you start or the *Vanodine* causes its own stains! This is repeated every day for as long as necessary. Masks are de-spotted, with tweezers, on the Wednesday before the show; a day when the birds are not sprayed. To prevent feather staining, pink iodine blocks are replaced by white ones and no greenfood is fed. Show cages are always cleaned as soon as they come back from a show and so they need only minor attention. We always prepare more than twice as many birds than we have entered so there is always a good choice when it come to making the final show team selection.

Jorge De Pina:

The feeding routine is the same as in the breeding season. In a hot climate and when tasks are being carried out by staff it is essential to have a system. We are always spraying Budgerigars: it keeps things cool. Spraying does much to assist new feathers to come through more quickly and they seem to open up much better. We spray with cold water up until five days before a show. Any special foods, such as greenfood, carrot and softfood is withheld from the same day to prevent faces from being stained. The servants continue with the routine work but I tend to be very active myself during show preparation time. I find that I see things that no member of staff, no matter how dedicated, will notice. If any feathers are damaged I carefully remove them. Broken flights and tails are the biggest problem and these are removed as a matter of course rather than at any stage in the show preparation. Excess spots are removed (by being pulled) midweek before the show. This timing gives the feathers time to fall back to their natural position and so avoids leaving a gap in the mask. Cages are always kept clean as a matter of routine, but at show time it is more important than ever. When Budgerigars are taken to shows in Brazil we do not have to bother with show cages. These are provided by the organising society. The exhibits are transported to and from the show in carrying boxes. At the end of the show, servants are employed to clean all of the show cages. It is not unknown for me to enter a team of 150 Budgerigars. If they had to be transported in show cages and all those cages had to be cleaned after every show it would be a daunting prospect.

The week before a show proceeds to the following programme:

Sunday: A heavy spray of cold water is given. A show cage, containing corn, oats and a *Trill* stick, is attached to the stock cage.

Monday: Spray with water containing Johnson's *Plumespray* and baby shampoo.

Tuesday: Stop special foods. Just seed, oats and *Trill* sticks.

Wednesday: Diet remains the same. Excess mask spots are pulled. (no spraying after this)

Thursday: Any bird with blood on its head is washed with cold water.

Friday: Pin feathers are opened by rubbing between fingers or gently with the back of a knife blade. The last job, before leaving for the show is to put the birds into travel boxes.

John Woods:

The general management routine during the show season is virtually the same as during the breeding season, except that instead of inspecting nest-boxes I attend to the show team. Most of the work is done when they are caught up from the flights to be housed in stock cages. Broken tails and flights are removed at this stage and, if necessary, faces are washed. From time to time replacements have to be brought into the show team and these are treated in the same way. Regular spraying with cold water is carried out in conjunction with show cage training.

The light spraying of most of my show team continues up until the middle of the last week before the show. However, birds that require a little extra preparation are sprayed right up until the day before the show. Masks are trimmed around Wednesday, just before the last general spraying. Bent tails and flights are straightened by being dipped in very hot water (being very careful to make sure that it is only feathers that enter the water), smoothed down and then put under the cold tap to harden off the feathers in their new position.

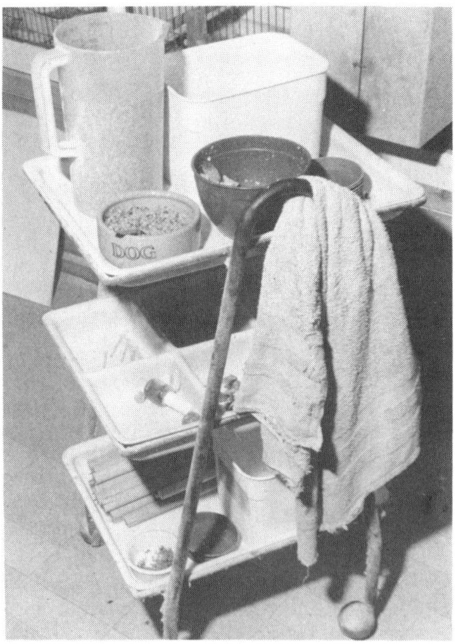

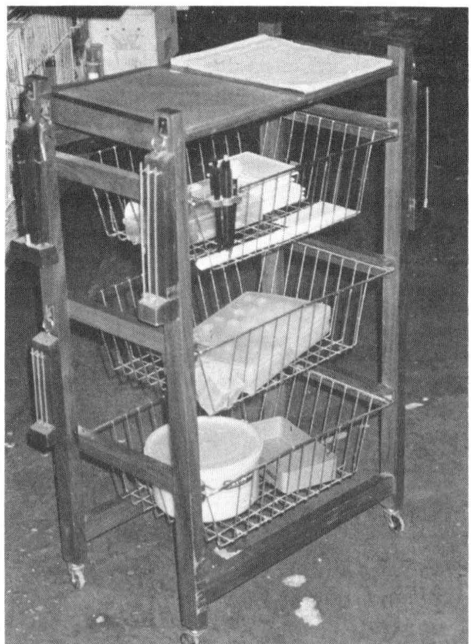

Oceans apart they might be, but top Budgerigar breeders arrive at the same solution to ease the management of their studs. Both John Woods in England (left) and Jorge De Pina in Brazil (right) find a trolley invaluable as they go about their birdroom tasks.

CHAPTER 3

FEEDING

How do you feed your Budgerigars?

Jim Moffat:

Basic seed mixture:

My Budgerigars' basic diet consists of Trill with added plain canary seed. I buy the plain canary locally and do not go into details about where it was grown. I have used more or less the same mixture for many years. There have been slight variations as feeding fashions have changed, but I always return to the basic diet described.

Extras:

When breeding pairs have youngsters they are provided daily with dry groats, Budgerigar tonic seed and a proprietary softfood (EMP dampened with water to make it crumbly). I used to feed soaked oats but these sometimes became sour when I was away from home. When feeding any soaked seeds it is important to clean dishes regularly. Soaked seed also resulted in dirtier, smellier nest-boxes. It may have also resulted in more chicks, but the "dry seed" routine suits my method of management. I used to feed wild greenfood when I had time to gather it. Rye grass is one of the best foods you can offer Budgerigars. Time not withstanding, the risk of pollution makes feeding wild greenfood a risky practice today.

Drinking water:

I have now installed a water filter so that I can provide my Budgerigars with purer drinking water. We have a filter system in the house now and the water is certainly more palatable. As far as the Budgerigars are concerned I have heard it said that we can purify water too much! We really do not know enough about the detailed needs of small birds.

Additives:

I add both Cytacon and Abidec to the drinking water constantly; at the rate a teaspoonful of Cytacon and 16 drops of Abidec to two gallons (9 litres) of water.

Grit and minerals:

Mineralised grit is always available and topped up every week. Cuttlefish bone and iodine nibbles are also provided.

The feeding arrangement in a Snell cage. Tonic seed, plain canary seed and grit in separate dishes plus a bunch of chickweed.

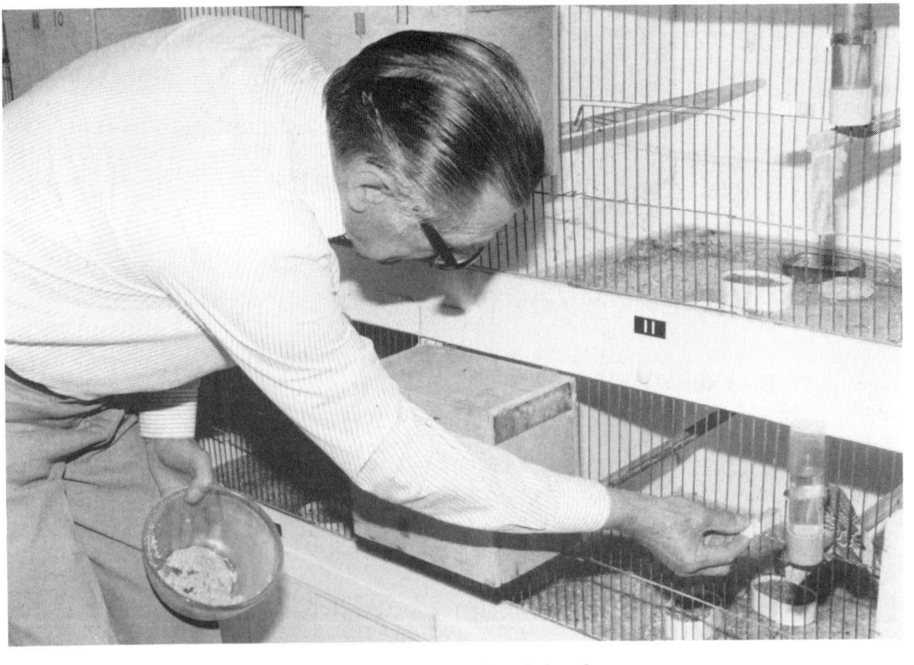

Arthur Snell feeds carefully-prepared softfood.

Chris and Arthur Snell:

Basic seed mixture:

All the seed we feed comes from Haiths. It is a local firm, at Cleethorpes, so we know all of the people there. We feed in open dishes; one containing "Rayreen" Mazagan canary seed and the other a mixture of three parts tonic seed, two parts white millet and one part panicum. Haiths tonic seed has been improved recently by including safflower seeds in the mixture and omitting dried spinach.

Extras:

Our breeding pairs receive many extras. Brown wholemeal bread is damped with a lactose-free baby milk ("Wysoy") made up at the rate of 10 scoops to a $1\frac{3}{4}$ pints (1 litre) of water with a scoop of glucose powder added. This is fed every evening from the 16th day after the first egg was laid until chicks leave the nest. All birds, including those in the flights receive eggfood which consists of eight hard-boiled eggs, four medium-size carrots (grated), a pinch of salt and enough bran to bring the mixture to a fluffy texture. Dry millet sprays and soaked oats are supplied regularly. Seeding grasses and chickweed are fed in large quantities whenever they are available. During the show season no bread and milk is offered and soaked oats are fed only to those members of the show team which we feel would benefit from putting on a little more weight.

A block with a stout wire protruding from it is ideal for keeping such "extras" as carrots and sweet corn from getting dirty on a cage floor. These are the type used in the De Pina birdroom.

Drinking water:

Chris's birds used to receive filtered water, but now all the birds' drinking water comes straight from the tap.

Additives:

The only additive used is Cytacon in the drinking water twice a week. Arthur used Entrodex prior to last breeding season and this could have helped them to reach a high peak of breeding fitness.

Grit and minerals:

Haiths mineral grit, Liverine iodine nibbles, cuttlefish bone and old mortar (for the lime it contains).

Jorge De Pina:

Basic seed mixture:

Things are hard in this country and you need a basic diet that you can have confidence in, so I use the standard mixture marketed by Trill of South America. We have a good working relationship. I am successful and they support me. Having said that, the bird seeds available in Europe are better than those we can obtain in Brazil. For example, our plain canary is much smaller; more like grass seed. I give the best I can obtain and accept that I have to compensate for my Budgerigars' nutritional needs by feeding extras.

Extras:

The softfood mixture (fed every day) consists of soya milk, wheat germ flour, yeast, powdered oats, flour, honey, sweet corn, carrot, banana, eggs, wheat germ oil, cod liver oil and "Kaliamon B12" (calcium + vitamin B12) This is so nutritious that I would have no hesitation in feeding it to my children. The improvement with birds on this diet is remarkable. They put on weight (muscle not fat), feather condition improves and they are much fitter all round. The Budgerigars I bring back from the UK seem to put on muscle and their feather quality improves after the first moult while being fed on my system. By European standards my softfood mixture is wet and, because I keep a record of what every pair consumes, the quantities fed are quite small. They only get what they need. Dry oats, groats and small sunflower seeds are also used to put weight on any Budgerigar that needs it. Carrot or spinach (no wild greenfood) is fed once a week. I feed lots of sweetcorn; it grows all the year round in Brazil and the birds love it. I have a sack delivered every week and keep them in the fridge. Four times a week I cut each cob into three or four pieces and fix a piece onto a wire fixed into a block which stands on the floor of each cage. This arrangement prevents the corn from being soiled and the blocks are washed at the end of each day.

Drinking water:

Water is filtered and renewed every day.

Additives:

"Entrodex" probiotic is fed whenever there is possibility of stress; for example: five days before a show and five days after. It contains beneficial, live bacteria and a nutrient which feeds these and other bacteria in the gut. They let a bird bring itself to health and fitness. Since introducing Entrodex my birds have seemed fitter and there are fewer "little" problems in the birdroom.

Grit and minerals:

Grit come from a clean, local beach. It is rich in salt and oystershell so there is no need to make cuttlefish bone available.

John Woods:

Basic seed mixture:

I feed my Budgerigars a continental mixture which offers an excellent variety of seeds. However, like all the continental mixtures I know, it does not contain enough plain canary or white millet to meet my requirements in the breeding season. The mixture is made by Bayers of Belgium and contains: plain canary, white millet, yellow millet, red Dakota millet, panicum millet and small amounts of hemp, niger and groats. I feed the mixture as received during the summer but in the breeding season I add 26lbs (12 kg) of Bayers plain canary and 13lbs (6kg) of white millet to each 55lbs (25 kg) sack of mixture. I believe in feeding a wide variety of seeds but consider that the seeds I add are of prime importance when Budgerigars are breeding.

Extras:

I use EMP eggfood which is of good quality, easy to use and readily taken by the birds. Pairs with chicks receive this morning and evening. They also receive a little brown bread soaked with milk in the evening. In the winter my birds get a slice of carrot twice a week and young, tender dandelion leaves in the spring. I also pick seeding heads of dandelions before the seed pods burst. My Budgerigars love these. In summer there is chickweed but I feed this in only small amounts because I do not like any to be left on the floor of the flight at the end of the day.

Drinking water:

I always use filtered water.

Additives:

After the hens have laid I add Abidec multi-vitamin to the drinking water twice a week at the rate of three drops to one pint (0.57litres).

Grit and minerals:

Mineral grit is always available. Also Kilpatrick's Pigeon minerals, cuttlefish bone and a lump of old black mortar, which the birds sharpen their beaks on as well as picking at the lime which is one of the mortar's ingredients. In the flights there are cattle licks (salt blocks) which are well used and the flight floors are strewed with sand.

CHAPTER 4

MEDICATION

What do you look for when checking your birds' health and what do you do about it?

Jim Moffat:

Sick Budgerigars are easily spotted. They are usually sitting fluffed up and looking unhappy. Even after all the trials and tribulations of keeping Budgerigars for more than 50 years I am still not confident when treating sick birds. Over the years I have tried the medications that were in fashion but some birds still died and the ones that recovered may well have done so without treatment. I remain confused as to the correct remedies and this is not helped by still not having found a vet who is skilled at treating the various illnesses encountered. Apart for isolating them and keeping them warm I do not administer treatment.

Chris and Arthur Snell:

Any bird that is not well is quickly spotted. If just fluffed up they are placed in a small cage and kept warm on top of a boiler in the house. Care must be taken to ensure that a bird does not become dehydrated. If there is no apparent improvement an antibiotic is given. If a bird's droppings are green we administer Johnson's *Avol.* For clogged vents, we gently remove the excreta and wash with a solution of *Vanodine V18.* If there is no improvement within 24 hours two drops of *Mysteclin* (a combined antibiotic and fungicide) are administered every day for three days. A local vet is very helpful.

Jorge De Pina:

It is easy for an experienced breeder to spot any behaviour changes. Things to watch out for are: fluffed up, softfood (or even seed husks) around the face, droppings different from normal, soiled vents, regurgitation of seed (other than normal breeding behaviour), feathers of the head or face sticky. *Mysteclin* is wonderful for treating this last condition. It is not manufactured any more in liquid form but a friend in England gets it made up specially through a vet. With him and the vet I can get everything

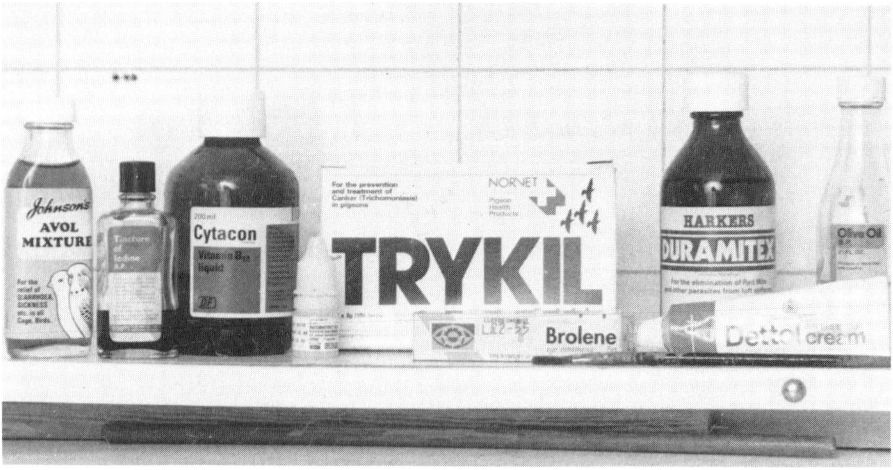

There are many products, useful in the Budgerigar birdroom, which can be obtained without a prescription. Even so it helps if you can get to know a vet who understands the special needs of Budgerigars.

required for the medicinal needs of my birds. I do not like giving antibiotics unless it is really necessary. Ninety-five per cent of sick birds recover just by being kept warm. I wash the vent, if necessary, and move the bird to my small hospital room, always with one or two other Budgerigars. They need friends, particularly when they are not feeling well. I feed corn every day and try to avoid having to give medication, but if an antibiotic is needed I use terramycin. I believe that "going light" is a symptom of several different diseases rather than a disease in its own right. This is why different cases respond to different treatments. Eye problems are treated with *Neobiotic* drops, damaged skin with antiseptic cream, scaly face and scaly leg with *Ivomectin* (scaly leg is a much greater problem in Brazil than in the UK). *Vanodine V18* is used for all cleaning jobs except for softfood dishes which are soaked in *Milton.* Johnson's *Anti-mite* and *Anti-peck* are both used.

John Woods:

If I have a problem with a Budgerigar in the flights – looking fluffed up, being sick, having loose droppings or a soiled vent – I isolate the bird and keep a very careful eye on the flights to see whether any other bird shows the same signs. If so, I scrub out and disinfect the flights and the perches and add 5ml of terramycin to one pint (0.57litres) of drinking water. The occasional bird that has a clogged vent is treated very carefully. It may not have been able to defecate and so no pressure must be exerted on the bird's lower regions. I make a solution of warm water and borax and, holding the bird gently, immerse its lower end into the solution and let it soak. After the blockage has softened and broken up I clean the vent area thoroughly and trim away any long feathers. Finally, I dust with kaolin powder.

What does your birdroom's medicine chest contain?

Jim Moffat:

I do not have a medicine chest in my birdroom.

Chris and Arthur Snell:

Neobiotic drops for eye problems, *Mysteclin*, *Trykil*, tincture of iodine, *Avol*, a solution for treating candidiasis, nail clippers, sharp scissors, cotton and spare rings (for splayed legs).

Jorge De Pina:

Mysteclin, *Neobiotic* drops, *Ivomectin*, *Vanodine V18*, Johnson's *Anti-peck* and *Anti-mite*, *Milton*, *Trykil*, *Amprosol*, *Bulvermin* and terramycin.

John Woods:

Trykil, terramycin, chloromycetin, *Nystatin*, *Panalog* (for treating eyes), *Ivomectin*, witch hazel, olive oil, *Germolene*, iodine, boracic acid powder, kaolin powder, *Vaseline* and liquid paraffin.

Do you use medication on a routine, preventative basis?

Jim Moffat:

My birds are systematically treated with *Trykil* (Emtryl soluble) at the end of the breeding season to protect them against trichomoniasis.

Chris and Arthur Snell:

In November and June – before and after the breeding season – our birds are systematically treated with *Trykil* (Emtryl soluble) to protect them against trichomoniasis. We do not worm or administer antibiotics on a regular basis.

Jorge De Pina:

I dose with *Trykil* (Emtryl soluble) twice a year against trichomoniasis. I also dose all birds bought in the UK before shipping them to Brazil in an effort to avoid importing the problem to South America. I see lots of unfit Budgerigars in the UK. *Amprosol* is given twice a year against coccidiosis and my Budgerigars are wormed with *Bulvermin*, also twice a year.

John Woods:

My entire stock is treated with *Trykil* (Emtryl soluble) at the end of the breeding season and again six weeks before I pair up. This is the only preventative treatment I administer.

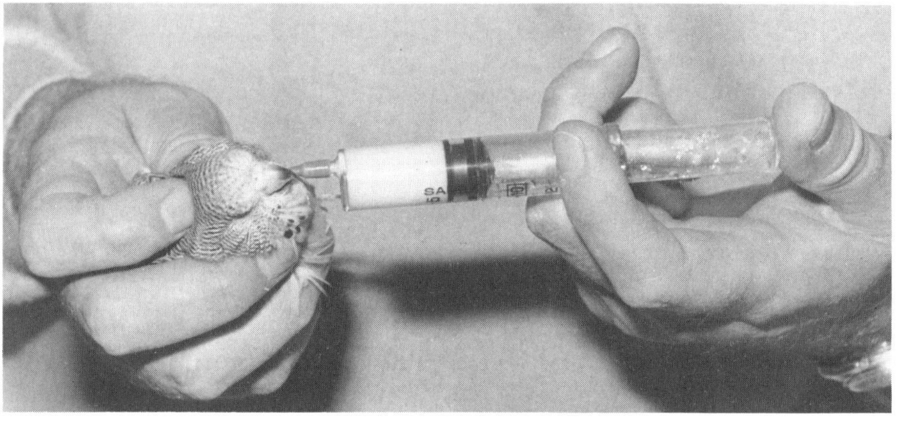

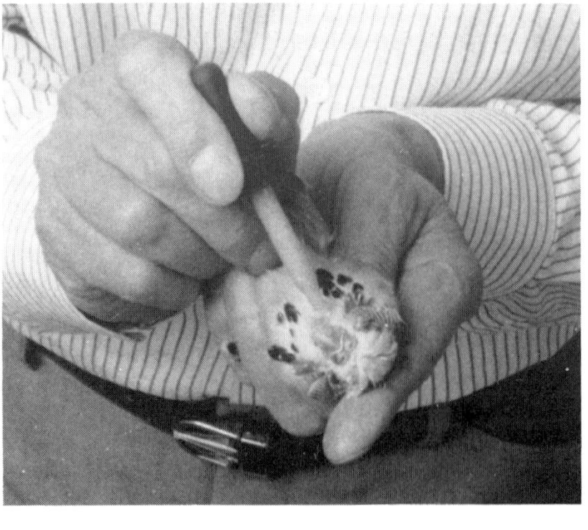

Two ways of hand-feeding chicks – or administering medicine. John Woods chooses a syringe (above) while Arthur Snell prefers a dropper (left).

CHAPTER 5

THEIR STUDS

(Readers who are not conversant with the genetics of colour expectation will find it helpful to refer to Chapter 7 when the experts discuss pairings that produce Greens).

How many Budgerigars do you keep and what varieties are they?

Jim Moffat:

I retain 48 pairs. This is probably too many, but I do believe you require to breed a few hundred chicks each year to give yourself the chance of producing a dozen or so outstanding youngsters. Ninety per cent of my Budgerigars are either Light Greens or Opaline Light Greens, with the bias very heavily towards the former. I like Dark factors, but have never set out to breed them and so only have one or two. The rest of the stud is made up of Grey Greens, Greys and Skyblues. I am not a Cinnamon man and, as will always happen in any stud these days, when a Cinnamon hen turns up in a

Chris and Arthur Snell usually breed between 400 and 500 youngsters each year. Housing them in nursery cages, like the one shown here, goes a long way towards steadying them down.

nest I soon dispose of it. I have pottered with other colours and varieties. Every pair I choose is with the intention of breeding Light Greens. My father kept Light Greens and that is another reason for me choosing them as a variety to keep.

Chris and Arthur Snell:

We usually breed between 400 and 500 youngsters and so by the end of the breeding season we can have 600 to 650 Budgerigars. About 60 per cent of our birds are Normal Light Greens. We also keep a number of Dark Greens, Opaline Greens, Blues, a few Greys, less Grey Greens, Cinnamons, Yellowfaces, Spangles and a couple of Dominant Pieds.

Jorge De Pina:

I keep between 600 and 700 Budgerigars and of these 350 to 400 are Normal Greens. Most of the rest are Normals of other colours, including Violets, and then there are Yellowfaces, Dominant Pieds, Spangles, Lutinos plus some Cinnamons, Opalines and Yellows.

John Woods:

The number of Budgerigars I keep as resident stock amounts to around 250. Of these about 25 per cent are Light Greens plus a handful of Dark Greens. About 10 years ago my Light Greens increased in numbers until they comprised approximately 80 per cent of my stud and the level remained the same for five or six years before reducing to the present proportion. When the Greens were at their most numerous my other two families of Budgerigar (one of Greys and Grey Greens and the other of Greys and Blues) became rather thin on the ground. This posed a problem because birds from these families had a very good show record: best breeder at Budgerigar World show with a Grey hen, best in show at Scottish BS with a Grey Green cock, best Grey Green at the BS Club Show and several other best in show and major awards. Rather than let them diminish further I decided to cut back on the number of Light Greens and have since made a concerted effort to bring the other two families up to their previous level. I have also added more Cinnamons and Opalines to my stud.

Which of the other varieties can improve your Greens?

Jim Moffat:

If you are setting out to breed Light Greens of quality there is no point in using anything other than Normals and Opaline hens. In truth, any Budgerigar that is good enough can help any stud, no matter what colour it is. In my experience, Opalines tend to be more prolific than Normals. They can also help in increasing spot size – and I like to see large spots on a Budgerigar. If I could breed 100 outstanding Light Greens every year I would not need to use any complementary colours such as Grey Greens and Skyblues.

Chris and Arthur Snell:

Other varieties can be used to complement or improve the feathering of Light Greens; with Grey Green and Skyblue being the best. We both agree that Grey Greens can improve feather texture but, on the whole, Skyblues would be our preference. Arthur believes that Blues improve the colour of Light Greens, but Chris is not entirely convinced. Opaline hens are very useful for improving spot size and Yellowfaces can be used to enrich the colour of Light Greens' faces. In our experience, Cinnamon is no help in improving feather texture.

Jorge De Pina:

I will use any colour of Budgerigar if I think it will improve my Light Greens. The best Grey Greens have good features that can help virtually any colour and I have no hesitation using Cinnamons or Opalines if they suit my purpose. When I began specialising in Greens I paid too much attention to numbers. I retained Greens just because they were Greens. I now regret selling certain Skyblues, Greys, Grey Greens, Opalines and Cinnamons which could have brought about a more rapid improvement in my Greens. The way I work is to concentrate on improving desirable features. I do not worry about keeping my stock in separate families when selecting breeding partners, so if I need to improve spot size and shape I will select the best-spotted most suitable mate, no matter what colour it might be. Usually this will be an Opaline because Opalines tend to excel in spot quality. I prefer to use Opaline hens with Normal cocks because this controls the Opaline factor by producing Normal hens and Normal split Opaline cocks. On the other hand, if you pair an Opaline cock with a Normal hen you finish up with all Opaline hens and Normal split Opaline cocks. Opaline hens are also very useful for improving shoulder, width and feather quality. In fact I would go as far as to say that Opaline hens are invaluable in the production of quality Light Greens. If it is good enough I will breed a Cinnamon with my Light Greens. Cinnamon is a strong variety and has much to offer, but it reproduces in the same way as Opaline and so one has to be careful to keep it under control if the objective is to breed top-class Normals. In an ideal world, I would have enough Normal hens not to have to use Opalines and Cinnamons. Thank God there is no such thing as a split Opaline or split Cinnamon hen! It is important to retain good, Normal hens of any colour and so you need to establish your requirements before deciding which birds can be sold. Accurate stock lists are important. It is no good finding that you have sold more hens than you should have and then trying to buy suitable replacements just before the breeding season begins. You will not get them. Budgerigars are my business and any business requires a good stock control system.

John Woods:

At one time it was the ambition of every Budgerigar breeder to have all of the birds in his stud looking the same. Those days are long gone. Nowadays breeding stock needs to be diverse in its composition in order to add a different dimension and greater scope to the choice of matings. In consequence, I will use any Budgerigar which, in my estimation, will result in an improvement - whatever its variety. In my opinion, this is the way to compete successfully on the show bench with the modern Budgerigar.

(above) The beautiful setting of Jim Moffat's birdroom; looking across the sea to the Isle of Arran.

(right) Replenishing the seed pots is the first job that John Woods undertakes as he tends each cage. (photographs: Les Lockey)

(above) Chris Snell makes a quick check of the birdroom as soon as he arrives home from work. He returns a little later to cater for his Budgerigars' needs, beginning with the inspection of nest-boxes.

(left) Arthur Snell has two birdrooms. The one shown here is of timber construction clad with plastic weatherboard, which creates a most attractive appearance. (photographs: Les Lockey)

A large group of Light Greens is a joy to behold. These are seen in one of the Snells' inside flights.

This outstanding pair of Light Greens are part of Chris and Arthur Snell's stud. Pairing Light Green to Light Green has the advantage of producing less non-Light Greens than other matings. It also produces good colour. (photographs: Les Lockey)

(left) Jorge De Pina feeds many "extras" to ensure that his Budgerigars' nutritional needs are met. He would have no hesitation in including the same foodstuffs in his children's diet.

(below) This Light Green cock, with its superb capping, is the sort of Budgerigar that takes major awards for Jorge De Pina at the leading shows in South America.

Size, good shoulders, depth of mask and feather quality are all features which are strengths in Jorge De Pina's Budgerigars. All these are displayed by this excellent Light Green cock which has taken several best in show awards for the De Pina stud. (photograph: Breda Fotografias)

This young Light Green cock, bred by John Woods, has not yet completed its moult. Even so, its outstanding potential shines through. (photograph: Les Lockey)

The peak of any UK breeder's achievement is to breed a Budgerigar which takes best in show at the Budgerigar Society Club Show. This outstanding Light Green cock did just that for John Woods in 1988. (photograph: Les Lockey)

Many of Jim Moffat's successes have been gained with hens, including best opposite sex at the BS Club Show. This one demonstrates that there is no possibility of Jim losing his touch.

Jim Moffat recommends using a Dark Green to maintain and even improve the colour of Light Greens – if you can find one good enough. This Dark Green cock, bred by Jim, would be an asset in any Light Green stud. (photographs: Les Lockey)

You do not have to be an expert to detect that this nest-feather Light Green cock bred by Jim Moffat (left) has the potential to be just as good as its outstanding adult relative pictured below. (photographs: Les Lockey)

Chris and Arthur Snell believe that among the strengths of their own stud are depth and width of face and mask. This Light Green cock, a worthy descendant of the hen that took the Supreme Trophy at the 1984 BS Club Show, confirms that belief. (photograph: Les Lockey)

Even though he has been reorganising his stud since his great win of 1988, John Woods is still producing Light Greens of this excellent quality. (photograph: Les Lockey)

Jorge De Pina's declared ambition is to build the largest and best stud of Light Green Budgerigars in the world. He looks forward to the day when he can bring Light Green cocks like this to compete with the best that Europe has to offer. (photograph: Fred Wright)

CHAPTER 6

ALL ABOUT GREENS

What is the attraction of Greens and is specialising a good idea?

Jim Moffat:

When I started, Light Greens were the top colour. They were the kings of the Budgerigar Fancy. Despite the different varieties that existed then and the new ones that have appeared since, Light Green is still my favourite variety. They were overtaken and dominated by Grey Greens for some years, but there are now Light Greens that can match any other variety for quality. Indeed, that is true of any Normal variety today. There are

Ninety per cent of Jim Moffat's Budgerigars are Light Greens and Opaline Light Greens, The rest of the stud is made up of Grey Greens, Greys and Skyblues. Some of them can be seen here in his large inside flight.

Jim Moffat says that he would like to produce large quantities of Light Greens with huge, box-like heads. This cock demonstrates that such Budgerigars are already in his stud.

excellent Grey Greens, Greys, Light Greens and Skyblues that are capable of taking best in show awards at the top shows. In my opinion it is a good idea to specialise in anything if your objective is to succeed and get to the top. Specialisation gives a greater choice of birds when it comes to choosing the show team and the breeding team. When choosing breeding partners a small variation in a particular feature can make a big difference to a bird's suitability. Having a large number of candidates to choose from helps to overcome the setbacks met by every Budgerigar exhibitor; such as dropped spots, broken tails and a general loss of show condition. I have persevered, and continue to persevere, with this colour and I suppose the target is to win best in show at the BS Club Show. Light Greens posed a challenge when I first took them up and they still do so, that and their appearance is their constant attraction.

Chris and Arthur Snell:

Obviously, achieving our first ever win with a Light Green and seeing the high quality Light Greens of Tom Rothery and Jack Fisher influenced our decision to keep them, but there is more to it than that. Light Green is the colour of wild Budgerigars, they are the originals; the aristocrats of the Budgerigar world. We were told that they would be difficult, that we would lose the quality. We tried, succeeded and still have them. Even so they provide a challenge in maintaining the size of spots, depth of mask and depth of colour. There is also a degree of wastage when Cinnamons, Blues and Opalines appear in the nests of Light Greens. Specialising is a good thing once you have established a stud of quality and are sure that you want to concentrate on a particular variety. Colour should only become a major consideration after quality has been fixed, but a flight full of Light Green Budgerigars is a thing of beauty.

Jorge De Pina:

When I started I had a large proportion of Light Greens and Skyblues. Both Light and Dark Greens attracted me because of their even, deep body colour and I bought a lot of Light Greens during my early visits to the UK. I quickly realised that they were a variety to get into. If I was going to keep Budgerigars full-time I might as well keep one of the strongest, most popular colours; one that would always sell. I love breeding Greens and when I win I prefer it to be with Greens. Money is certainly not my only consideration as far as the Fancy is concerned, but I must always keep it in mind. Henry Ford did not make cars just for the fun of it. He wanted something that would sell. I have set myself the target of having 80 to 90 per cent of my breeding cages occupied by pairs of Light Greens and to be able to sell top quality Cinnamons and Opalines because my Greens are even better. I want to exhibit in Europe - and win! I understand that the rules of the Budgerigar Society now permit overseas exhibitors to compete as long as they comply with the law. To take best in show at the BS Club Show, Budgerigar World, London & Southern Counties or Lancashire, Cheshire & North Wales would be wonderful. Specialising is more difficult than breeding a wide range of varieties. You need to bring everything together on one colour whereas the non-specialist can forget about colour and concentrate only on quality. I do not think anyone can understand Budgerigars fully until they have kept them for 10 years. Only then should specialisation be considered.

John Woods:

It was seeing the marvellous Budgerigars of Tom Rothery and Jimmy Kenyon that prompted me to begin keeping Light Greens. Their Light Greens displayed a superb combination of style and showmanship which seemed to complement and emphasise the beautiful contrast between the bright green body colour and the black and yellow markings. They really made a lasting impression upon me. It was my ambition to breed some which attained the same level of quality. Breeding a Light Green cock which was good enough to win the supreme award at the Budgerigar Society Club Show was just one step on the way. Having done that I now want to breed one even better. If I ever achieve that ambition I will want to improve on that. The challenge, to me, is a perpetual one. Within the Budgerigar Fancy everybody's circumstances are different. All one can do is their best under their particular circumstances. If a fancier's birdroom and facilities are limited then there is a good argument for specialising in his chosen variety rather than keeping a collection made up of lots of different varieties no one of which is strong enough to make any impact on the show bench. Specialising provides wide choice of breeding partners and plenty of back-up for the show team.

What makes a good – and a bad – Green?

Jim Moffat:

A good Green is a good Budgerigar and a good Budgerigar must be a big bird with an outstanding head and mask. It must have a good backline and an upright stance. It is highly desirable that its stance should carry it clear and above the perch. Deportment - style, swank, call it what you will - is very important. A carrot shape is essential and to achieve this a Budgerigar needs to have broad shoulders. To make a good Budgerigar a good Green, it needs to have a strong, deep, even, grass green body colour and clear, solid markings. Head flecking is a serious fault of markings as far as the show bench is concerned but, in my opinion, far less serious when it comes to breeding. If an outstanding Budgerigar was flecked I would have no hesitation in using it for breeding, though I would not pair it with another flecked Budgerigar. The most serious faults are: having a narrow, mean face, being small, having a drooping tail and very small spots.

Chris and Arthur Snell:

A super Budgerigar always has that bit of extra size so a good Light Green needs to be large, have a good position and, of course, be of the correct colour. There are many faults of exhibition Budgerigars, among them: lack of deportment, narrow head, narrow face, lack of shoulders, short mask, crossed wings, dipped tail, protruding beak, lacking size, poor back line, size and shape of spots and poor colour. A Light Green's body colour should be grass green; not too light and not too dark. Any good Budgerigar must have a good face and mask. No matter what the variety, a shallow mask

In Jim Moffat's view, a good Green must be a big bird with an outstanding head and mask, This Light Green cock, from his stud, certainly answers to that description.

detracts from a Budgerigar's quality. Spots are also important in that their size should be in proportion to the mask on which they are set. Large spots need a deep, wide mask. We take the Budgerigar Society standard as our guide to excellence.

Jorge De Pina:

First and foremost, a good Green must be a good Budgerigar with excellent head qualities, shoulders, cap and position on the perch. When describing a good Green I am visualising a Green in a show cage; one that is capable of taking top awards. It must be in the very best condition. A

Budgerigar that is out of condition displays only its potential quality. A good Green must have strong coloration. I hate to see poor colouring in Greens. I dislike head flecking but it cannot be ignored that many flecked Budgerigars display lots of other desirable qualities. Even more serious than flecking, in my opinion, are opalistic markings on Normal Greens. I hate seeing body colour on the backs of heads and necks, where yellow ought to be. This fault can become dominant in a stud of Normals and so is very difficult to control. This is one reason that the use of Opalines when breeding Normals calls for vigilance. Even worse, it can be another variety, such as Cinnamon, which introduces the problem. I like Budgerigars of substance; big Budgerigars, but they have to have good feather quality. Big, buff Budgerigars may have their place in the breeding cage but I do not see them as show winners. Too much coarse feathering can bring feather problems. The continual use of buff Budgerigars in the breeding cage results in birds that do not grow their flights or tails and have difficulty in flying. Other faults to be avoided are: dropped tail, large protruding beak, pointed narrow head, lack of shoulders (this fault guarantees a poor mask), poor back line (hollows and bumps), lack of size, small spots.

John Woods:

What makes a good Light Green? As with other varieties of Budgerigar it must be one with no obvious faults and well-endowed with the various exhibition features we require; features such as size, width of head, breadth of shoulder, depth of face and straightness of back. However, a Budgerigar can have all of these desirable features but it will still not be a winner unless it has style. I like to see a Budgerigar that stands up off the perch rather than slouching down on it. Generally speaking faults of shape can disqualify a bird from both the show and breeding teams, whereas faults of colour and markings – such as opalescence, uneven body colour, blue showing through the green and a degree of flecking – while making a Green unsuitable for exhibition are not so serious in the breeding cage as long as their partners are chosen with care. Light Greens should be a beautiful, rich, emerald green colour. Defining a bad one is not so easy. I think that one that has more faults to offer than good features would be a bad one. The sort of faults I am referring to are: too small in every department, short of backskull, hollow neck, nipped neck, hinged tail, bad all-round shape and poor colour.

Which faults are correctable and which are not?

Jim Moffat:

All of the faults I referred to above (lack of size, narrow face, drooping tail and lack of spots) are correctable by selective breeding; some more difficult than others. Lack of size would not automatically disqualify a Budgerigar from my breeding team as long as it was excellent in every other respect. A Budgerigar which is narrow and mean in the face has no place in any serious Budgerigar breeder's plans. A drooping tail is nearly as serious though I have known individuals that are so good they could be worth a second look. Small spots is perhaps the most easily cured fault of those mentioned. As mentioned earlier, Opaline hens can help in this respect. The problem with setting out to cure a fault is that it takes too long and so it is better not to use birds with such faults in your breeding programme. They certainly have no place in your show team! If your stud contains a fault which needs to be corrected it is necessary to go out and obtain outcrosses which display counter-balancing desirable features.

Chris and Arthur Snell:

Faults that can be corrected by careful selective breeding are poor colour and spots that are too small or misshapen – though these are easier to correct if the spots are in the correct position on the mask to start with. To improve a narrow face you first need to put broad shoulders onto a bird. Rather than saying that faults are not correctable we prefer to say that there are faults which would stop us using a particular Budgerigar in our breeding team. In this category are: narrow head, too much neck, dropped tail, protruding beak, small head and short mask. The last-mentioned is particularly difficult to correct.

Jorge De Pina:

It may seem all too easy to say: "Do not breed with Budgerigars that have major faults", but it is still an excellent rule to abide by. Of course, just how strictly you apply the rule can be affected by your level in the hobby. Champions should have reached the stage where they are refining finer points and should not be using poor quality Budgerigars with obvious faults. Novices and beginners have a different problem. They are making a start and can only use the birds that are at their disposal to best effect. It is like doing a jigsaw puzzle. It is a matter of getting all of the pieces in the right place. A champion with an established stud should have more pieces already in position and more to choose from. As far as specific faults are concerned, one to be avoided at all costs is the dropped tail. If one uses a Budgerigar with this fault you are building up problems for the future and so no matter how good a Budgerigar might be in other respects, one with a dropped tail should not be used for breeding. Budgerigars with large beaks are best avoided and should only be used if there is no other alternative. Budgerigars with lack of width between the eye seldom produce good chicks. A Budgerigar with a poor backline should be used only with care. Lack of overall size can be overcome by judicious selection of pairings, as can lack of body length. Spots are easy to increase in size. That is where Opaline hens prove their value. Head flecking has caused an over-reaction among some UK breeders and I have much to thank those frightened fanciers for. The flecked Budgerigars they have released to me have had so many good features that they have played a part in improving my stock. I say "thank you" now! Pairing a flecked Budgerigar with a clean, underspotted mate does much to control the problem.

John Woods:

The hinged tail is one of the worst problems. This can be passed on from generation to generation, sometimes in hidden form. Then, it can reappear when you think that you have got rid of it. The other main problems that a difficult to correct are – if they are correctable at all – the "faults of shape": things like lack of backskull, hollow or nipped-in neck or humped back. These are hard work. The "not enough of" faults are the easiest to improve: features such as spots not large enough, not quite enough depth of colour and not enough width. With these, one is trying to add something, to make a straight improvement and not trying to get rid of a fault that can remain hidden in the stock to re-emerge many years later.

What do you think of other breeders' and other countries' Greens? Are there any features that you would like to improve on your own?

Jim Moffat:

The strength of my own stud of Light Greens is their head quality and depth of mask. However, I would like to be able to produce greater quantities of Light Greens with huge, box heads and bursting with style. There are now a dozen or so top specialist breeders in the UK whose Budgerigars I admire for various reasons. They are highly successful on the show bench because their birds are superbly fit. I admire fanciers who manage to train their Budgerigars so that they appear to be tame when in a show cage. Good staging and frequent showing helps. The only first-hand experience I have of Light Green from other countries came when I visited Jo Mannes in Germany. I was very impressed by the quality of many of his Light Greens. The quality required to win with a Light Green Budgerigar in the 1990s is far higher than that of the ones I used to win with 30 and 40 years ago. The Budgerigar of all varieties in that era were much smaller all round. Harry Bryan was the dominant breeder of the period and almost unbeatable.

Chris and Arthur Snell:

We believe that the strengths of our own stud are depth and width of face and mask. When the feature "mask" is discussed, some breeders take it as meaning only the spots. It needs to be explained that we interpret the mask of a Budgerigar as being the yellow area of the face upon which the spots are located – an important distinction. Our stud also has the ability to produce good hens. We would like to improve the spot size on some of our Light Green cocks and to achieve more directional feathering over the eye. In the early 70s, Jack Fisher's Greens stood out from the rest. Then, in the mid-70s Ormerod & Sadler had some super Normals. From today's crop of breeders we admire many of the features displayed by Dave Topliss's Budgerigars. As far as the overseas scene is concerned, the Light Greens we have seen in the USA, Germany and Switzerland were not as good as the best that the UK has to offer though, at the time of writing, we had not visited Jo Mannes in Germany. The exhibition Budgerigar of the 1990s is far better than those of many years ago. Outstanding Budgerigars from 1970 onwards were Jack Fisher's Grey cock that took best breeders at the BS Club Show in that year, Ormerod & Sadler's Dark Green cock which was best in show two years running, in 1975 and 1976, Havenand & Ruthven's Grey cock which emulated the feat in 1980 and 81. Barry Wild's Grey Green hen which did the double of best in show at the first Budgerigar World show and the BS Club Show in 1983 and Taylor & Smith's Light Green cock which took the top award at the Budgerigar Society's Convention '90.

Jorge De Pina:

The strengths of my Greens are size, good shoulders, depth of mask and feather quality. The last-mentioned brings good colour and good fertility. I would like to improve spot size just a little and increase the feather slightly in the face. Greater use of Opalines would probably do the trick but I am cautious about any faults they might introduce. Other breeders' Greens that stick in my memory are all from the UK. There was Steve Bailey's 1987 cock (I bought it from Mick Joines and it bred some wonderful chicks for me), Steve Robertson's 1987 cock which I was not able to buy, Yorkshireman Bill Nichols' cock which I also bought. John Woods' best in show at the BS Club Show was a super Light Green and Chris and Arthur Snell consistently produce Light Green hens with good shoulders and substance. When I was in the USA a couple of years ago there were not so many good Light Greens, but Watkins and Miller had the best I saw. While judging in Switzerland I detected that their Light Greens are improving quickly. Budgerigar exhibiting is fairly new in Peru but, no doubt, we will also see rapid improvements there.

John Woods:

My stud does not excel in any specific, single feature. My strength is in having good all-round Budgerigars which breed year after year with no particular faults appearing. For some time I have been working on increasing spot size and have succeeded on a number of birds, but it takes a long time to spread a desirable feature such as this through the entire stock. I have always admired the Light Greens of Jim Moffat. He always puts out a very good team at the BS Club Show. I visited his birdroom two or three years ago and was impressed by the depth of quality displayed by both his Light Greens and Grey Greens. Two outstanding Budgerigars from the past that stick in my mind are the Dark Green cock of Ormerod & Sadler which took the best in show award at the BS Club Show two years running and Jim Moffat's Light Green hen which was awarded the best opposite sex in show trophy at the same event. These were, as the saying goes, years ahead of their time – but time moves on and the top Budgerigars have progressed so much in the last 10 years that these big winners from the past would not be in contention at today's top shows.

What is the best way of breeding a good Green?

Jim Moffat:

To breed a good Budgerigar you need to start with a good cock and a good hen. It is all down to the Budgerigars concerned being good enough visually and having excellent pedigrees. Preferably they will come from your own bloodlines, that have proved that they are dominant for their desirable features. They should come from families that have produced Budgerigars of show quality in the past. If I have the good fortune to produce a "stormer" from a particular pair, I keep the same pairing in successive breeding seasons. As far as producing Light Greens in numbers is concerned, Light Green to Light Green must be the favoured pairing and, in my experience, if the partners are good enough you will not lose any desirable qualities; physical or of colour and markings. As far as richness of body coloration is concerned I have not detected any difference between Light Greens that have been bred from Grey Greens, Greys or Skyblues. Neither does the use of Opalines have any adverse effect. The occasional use of a Dark Green – if you can find one good enough – can help to maintain and even improve the body colour of Light Greens. If I had enough good Budgerigars to permit me to make every pairing Light Green to Light Green I would think I had arrived in Paradise. When it comes to relationships, my favourite pairing is cousin to cousin. Of all the many combinations I have tried, this is the most prepotent and consistent in the quality of progeny produced. Grandparent to grandchild has produced some good Light Greens for me but closer pairings such as half-brother to half-sister have not proved so good. I have never paired as close as father to daughter or mother to son and I cannot think that these would be as good as my favourite cousin to cousin.

A busy breeding cage in the Moffat establishment.

Chris and Arthur Snell:

Light Green to Light Green has the great advantage that it produces less wastage; less non-Light Greens. This pairing also produces good colour. An ideal pair is a cock with intermediate buff feathering and good backskull to a long, typey hen. Backskull is not so important in the hen though she should have a very good width of face and head. A breeding hen should look beautiful, not ugly. Having selected the pairing on its visual balance, pedigree then comes into play; not so much pure pedigree as making certain that both cock and hen's parents and grandparents were Budgerigars of good quality. A "sport" (a good-looking Budgerigar that comes out of poor quality stock) is no use at all. Sooner, rather than later its progeny will revert back to its low-quality ancestry. Faults as well as good points must always be kept in mind when checking pedigrees. On this basis, our stud is based on pedigree breeding but certainly not on line or inbreeding. We even try to avoid breeding as close as cousin to cousin. Recently, we have brought about improvements by outcrossing. It matters little where an outcross comes from. If it looks good and its parents and grandparents look good it must bring an improvement. We are always on the lookout for such outcrosses. There COULD be a place for a Cinnamon in our breeding team but only if it was a wonderful Budgerigar, and even then it would need to be a hen rather than a cock. It would certainly need to be much better than any prospective Light Green hen that we were considering pairing to the same cock. Skyblue paired with Dark Green is an interesting mating in that it produces both Dark Green and Light Green chicks. It is better that the Dark Green is not split Blue because it brings into play the fact that Dark Greens/Blue can be either Type I or Type II (the difference is explained in chapter 7, Colour Expectations). In our experience the best mating for producing exhibition Dark Greens is Light Green × Dark Green.

Jorge De Pina:

Light Green to Light Green is the best pairing if the pair is good enough, if only because it produces more Light Greens than other matings. However, everything has to be right if this sort of mating is to be used for generation after generation. Green to Blue is the next best. Then there is Light Green to Grey Green, but you have to hope that the Grey Green is a single factor so that Light Greens are produced in the first generation. Whatever the pairing, quality is my main consideration, but the wish to produce Greens is never far from my mind. I never pair specifically to breed Dark Greens but some always show up in the course of the breeding season – Cobalts too. The best are very nearly as good as my Light Greens and they broaden the scope when it comes to putting out a winning show team. Big Buff Budgerigars have their place, but I do not like to keep too many of them. Their coarse feathering prevents them from displaying good colour, many cannot fly after the first moult, they do not breed well and neither do they live as long. I have visited several studs and seen many Budgerigars roosting on the floors of the flights. That cannot be a good thing. So, as far as feather texture is concerned, I try to avoid pairing Buff with Buff. Intermediate Buff × intermediate Buff is the best pairing, followed by intermediate Buff × Yellow (fine-feathered). Greens are sometimes paired with the specialist varieties, but the objective is always to improve the latter. Pedigree is important, but I have watched studs in the UK using close pairings and they do eventually all look alike – but they lose size and problems (such as dead-in-shell) begin to appear. It may be a good thing to have all your Budgerigars looking alike, but not if it is because they all have the same faults! In my experience, it is when you cross Budgerigars from related pairs into unrelated bloodlines that you see a rapid improvement in quality. I am a confirmed "outcrosser".

John Woods:

Whenever I pair up Budgerigars it is with the intention of breeding good ones. Sometimes a particular pairing is the culmination of several years planning and successive pairings to arrive at a point where the

Whenever John Woods pairs up Budgerigars it is with the intention of breeding good ones. The quality displayed by this young Light Green cock shows that he succeeds.

plans come to fruition. Most of the Budgerigars that have won major prizes for me have been bred like that. Occasionally luck plays a part. At the start of the 1979 breeding season I had made successive pairings over a three week period and had arrived at a situation where one breeding cage remained to be filled. Still in the flight was the brother to my best Grey Green cock. I had been trying to sell this bird all summer for £15, but no-one would buy it. After consideration I paired him with an Opaline Cinnamon Grey Green hen with the intention of using the pair to foster the eggs and chicks from the better pairs, if it became necessary. They were not required to act as foster parents during the first round and so they reared three chicks of their own. One of those three took the best breeder in show award at the 1979 Lancashire, Cheshire & North Wales BS area championship!

I have no dogmatic ideas when arranging the breeding programme or selecting pairings. My own findings, when it comes to pairing other varieties with Light Greens with the intention of breeding Light Greens, are as follows. I like a good Dark Green for its own attractiveness: they are beautiful Budgerigars. However, my main use for a good Dark Green is maintain the depth of colour of my Light Greens. A quality Grey Green (single factor) can make a very good mate for a Light Green. They seem to improve the body bulk of the Light Green youngsters produced. Based on my own experience, I would not recommend using Skyblues to breed Light Greens and I would certainly never use a Cobalt. No doubt there has been many a good Light Green bred from Blues but I feel that there is a loss of colour quality. To me there is nothing worse than a Budgerigar which looks three-quarters a Light Green and a quarter a Cobalt. As far as relationships are concerned, my favourite mating is grandfather to grand-daughter, but if the birds concerned are particularly well suited I would pair father to daughter or mother to son though this would be a one-off exercise and no other close pairings of this particular family would be undertaken for at least three years after.

How would you advise a newcomer to Greens to set up a successful stud?

Jim Moffat:

If I was a newcomer setting up a stud, I would put myself in the hands of a couple of successful breeders of sound reputation and try to listen to their advice. It would be best to start with a modest, planned, spending budget and not to deviate from it. It is all too easy to be carried away in your enthusiasm for a new hobby and to spend more than you intend – only to find that the Budgerigars you have bought are not going to help you in your quest to set up a successful stud of exhibition Budgerigars. Modest Budgerigars from good-quality families will give you a better than even chance of breeding better than themselves. There is one advantage in choosing Greens. There are always more Greens on the market than other colours. Too many newcomers visit an established champion's birdroom, point at his best Budgerigar and ask how much it will cost. You would be far better investing the money available in buying ten birds than one. Budgerigars – particularly good ones – tend to be relatively short-lived and if your single purchase should die you will soon leave a hobby which can be very rewarding. The better a Budgerigar is the more difficult it is to breed from so it is better to make your mistakes (and you will make mistakes!) with modest stock. Six to eight pairs will be quite sufficient for you to serve your apprenticeship: to learn how to look after and breed Budgerigars to best effect. Having got started, there would be a need to bring in better quality outcrosses in subsequent years to ensure that positive progress is made.

According to Chris and Arthur Snell, a good Budgerigar needs to have not only outstanding physical features, but should also possess an excellent pedigree. This Light Green cock, from their stud, has both.

Chris and Arthur Snell:

We would advise starting with 10 to 12 pairs. Greens should be the main objective but, at this stage, you may well have to use Grey Greens, Greys, Skyblues and Opalines. Try to pair Normal Green cocks with Normal or Opaline hens. Flecked Budgerigars are a problem for newcomers. They are often the best Budgerigars on offer in a seller's birdroom and so are tempting. We would not advise a newcomer never to buy a flecked bird because so many of them have so much to offer in other respects. However, care must always be taken with how it is used in the breeding programme. Never pair two flecked Budgerigars together or you will be building up trouble for the future by inbreeding a fault which can be difficult to eradicate. It would be best if you could get all the initial stock from one breeder but a good compromise is two breeders who have related stock. You must buy from someone you trust. The decision of who to buy from is as important as which birds to buy. The person should be capable of winning with his own birds and his stud must be fertile. In the first season breed as many chicks as you can, keep the best and sell the remainder – remembering that you need to retain approximately twice as many hens as cocks; particularly young hens. It is a mistake to let the average age of your stud increase. Indeed it demonstrates that you have not made progress. Plough all the income into a "bird-buying" fund and pay for seed etc. out of your own pocket. After three years your birdkeeping should be self-financing.

Jorge De Pina:

I believe that you need at least 12 pairs of the best Budgerigars you can find – Greens if possible. You should take into account the colour expectations that will result from using Cinnamons and Opalines when buying. If you know what a good Budgerigar should look like, buy from several breeders and decide who to buy from by getting around the big shows. Breed as many as possible and retain only the best, but do not be too hasty to make decisions about what to let go as some Budgerigars develop slowly – a fact you can turn to your advantage when buying! Before buying in the second year decide what feature it is you need to improve. If your birds have good head but lack spot size, it is spot size you should be buying, not heads. While letting quality come first you should also be thinking in terms of breeding Greens. Whether you succeed or not will, in the end, depend upon how dedicated you are. Buying is a skill. Lessons should be available in how to buy Budgerigars. A fancier who does not sell good Budgerigars to other breeders is unlikely to sell them to you. A fancier who is doing well with Budgerigars he has acquired from a top breeder is usually worth buying from. A breeder who will never sell a good bird is hardly worth wasting time on but an aviary visit is never a complete waste of time. Even if you cannot get hold of the Budgerigars you want you are almost certain to learn something.

John Woods:

The minimum number of Budgerigars a beginner should start with is three pairs because the objective is to be successful and to build up a stud, rather than an unrelated collection. If you are determined to breed Greens I recommend that they should all be purchased from one successful breeder of Greens. There is no need to buy "good" birds at this stage. If you buy the worst Budgerigars from a successful stud for a modest price (say three or four times the cost of a pet for each bird) the quality will come out in the progeny. They will surely breed better than themselves. If the breeder is "worth his salt" he will continue his interest in what happens to the birds and their progeny long after the beginner has left his birdroom. It is the experienced breeder who will match the pairs and should help the beginner to assess and sort out the youngsters produced in the first breeding season. He should also advise on the pairings for the second breeding season, which should be chosen from the birds available. Ideally there should be no need to bring in extra Budgerigars at the end of the first season. The end of the second breeding season should be a time of self-examination. The beginner should assess the progress made in two years, question his commitment to the hobby and decide where he is going. Only then can he decide upon his next move; whether to seek further advice, bring in an outcross aimed at moving the stud forward – or changing to another hobby. A general rule is to breed your own hens as it is far easier to buy a cock of quality.

How important is it for you to ring chicks at the earliest possible time?

Jim Moffat:

Unfortunately, the ring issue date is a case of the tail wagging the dog. My Budgerigars (and those of a lot of other breeders) come into breeding condition in October and so a ring issue date of November 1st, rather than January 1st, would encourage the breeding of Budgerigars.

Chris and Arthur Snell:

The ring issue date of January 1st poses no problems to us. We do not pair up our birds until early January and many of our best breeding results come in March and April. We never have chicks in the nest waiting for the rings to arrive. We pair our birds when they are in breeding condition regardless of the date. Breeding Budgerigars is far more important to us than the show season. Winning a show has never improved a Budgerigar.

Jorge De Pina:

In Brazil, our breeding season runs from June until the end of the year. All of the chicks can then be exhibited in the young bird classes for the whole of the following year. So 1992 ringed chicks are classed as breeders in 1993. This means that there is no rush to ring chicks and no hurry to get youngsters through the moult and out onto the show bench. This is a far better way of showing young Budgerigars than that employed in the UK.

Many UK breeders pair up their Budgerigars when they are fit, in October. This means that many excellent youngsters never get exhibited in the breeders' classes, which is a great pity.

John Woods:

If you are serious about exhibiting your Budgerigars, you need to have youngsters which are as mature as possible if they are to have a chance of winning at the early shows. If I am showing my Budgerigars I like to give them as great a chance of winning as possible. This means breeding early, if the birds are fit, and ringing chicks early in the year.

How do you go about acquiring stock of the required quality?

Jim Moffat:

It is not easy to purchase outcrosses of high quality. It is a phenomenon of the Budgerigar Fancy that a bird can take on a wholly unrealistic price just because a certain person is interested in buying it. However, in the past, I have made some successful exchanges; particularly with Gerald Binks. Exchanging birds is all about mutual trust between the people concerned.

Chris and Arthur Snell:

It is always difficult. We have gone out of our way to purchase Budgerigars we want but it has never been easy or particularly successful. Our best outcrosses have come from exchanges and the best opportunities to exchange have been unexpected. You must be ready to buy or exchange if the chance is there. We tend not to be interested in acquiring over-year hens because the only reason for bringing in new blood is to breed from it.

Jorge De Pina:

I go to the UK every year and buy "features" from fanciers in all the sections. Beginners and novices have very good Budgerigars there; many having spent big money with the top champions. It is only fanciers that are allocated status, their birds do not know whether they belong to a champion or a beginner. I buy groups of birds from different fanciers and bring just under 200 back to Brazil every time I visit there. I keep the best for myself and sell the rest to other South American breeders to try to cover my travelling expenses. Even though I have fanciers waiting for me to return with the "English" Budgerigars they have not been easy to sell in recent years because of the recession.

John Woods:

I believe it to be a good policy to bring in outcrosses on a regular basis – and therein lies a problem. It is not usually possible to purchase a Budgerigar of the quality I am looking for. One reason is that so many top-class Budgerigars have gone abroad over the past few years. I have to make exchanges with other breeders, which is often a risky business. The problem with that is that in order to make a fair exchange I have to let a Budgerigar go which I would prefer to retain. One of the considerations when deciding whether I want a particular Budgerigar is whether its quality can be seen in the rest of its family.

Do you ever sell the best Greens from your stud?

Jim Moffat:

I seldom sell my very best Light Greens. The top birds are very hard to produce and I enjoy looking at them. Seeing an outstanding, sensational youngster leave the nest is a great stimulus to keep on trying. They bring hope for the future.

Chris and Arthur Snell:

No. When we have good Greens our ambition is to breed even better ones from them. We are prepared to sell good Budgerigars if we have already bred from them and have younger birds to fill the gap they would otherwise leave.

Jorge De Pina:

I have no wish to sell my best Budgerigars. I need to sell birds to live, but the best ones are retained for me to exhibit and breed with.

John Woods:

I never sell my best Budgerigars. If one did, how could one make improvements?

What, in your opinion, is the degree of difficulty of Greens?

Jim Moffat:

There is no particular difficulty in breeding Light Greens. The difficulty is in producing large, show-quality youngsters in numbers. Over the years I have bred some outstanding, large, Light Green hens that have never produced a youngster. At the same time, their slighter, less-imposing sisters have bred very well. Outstanding hens are very vulnerable and seldom prolific. Although I have heard it said that the Dark factor detracts from substance and stature I have never found this to be true. I have benched the winner of the Dark Green cock class at the BS Club Show and the Budgerigar concerned was no more difficult to produce or to breed from than its Light Green counterparts. It is not unknown for some families to produce better Dark Greens than Light Greens. It is a genetical trait.

Chris and Arthur Snell:

Right from the start, people were telling us that Light Greens were a difficult variety to breed to exhibition standards. We have never found them to be so, though being a Normal variety they sometimes suffer from carrying other mutations in split form. It is frustrating to pair two Greens together and to breed chicks of an entirely different colour. Arthur believes that pairing Green to Green for generation after generation reduces size, but Chris believes that if the Greens are good enough this will not happen.

Jorge De Pina:

I am sure that Light Greens are not as difficult as some other varieties, such as Lutinos and Recessive Pieds.

John Woods:

It is a matter of degree. If left to choose their own mate any variety will regress, but it is certainly easier to breed good Light Greens than some of the more recessive varieties, such as Clearwings and Recessive Pieds. On the other hand it is easier to breed Grey Greens of high quality than Light Greens. Their grey green coloration has a wonderful way of hiding colour faults which would stand out on a Green. The darker you go the worse quality tends to be. There have been a few excellent Dark Greens bred over the years, but there have been far more good Light Greens. I would not even consider using an Olive in my breeding programme. They pull the other colours down so much. A good Olive is a Budgerigar in a million.

Are there any tactics that can help you win with Greens?

Jim Moffat:

When I used to exhibit my Light Greens every other weekend it sorted out many a problem. I soon found out which individuals chewed up their tails when housed in a show cage or spent the whole day of the show on the show cage floor. These could be eliminated from the show team for future events. It became easy to recognise natural showmen and to find out which judges liked which type of Budgerigar. If you found a judge who appreciated the kind of Budgerigar you were breeding it made sense to exhibit at the shows where they were adjudicating. There is nothing underhand or illegal in that. Exhibiting at only one show a year makes it a chancier business. All you can do is put out the best team available in the best possible condition. To exhibit a Budgerigar to best effect it must be in superb condition and staged in a faultless show cage. If a Budgerigar is confident, stylish and visually outstanding it will appeal to most judges. After that, it needs a degree of good fortune to go on and win best in show. I would enter as many as seven in the same class if I felt they had a chance of being in the tickets.

Jorge De Pina believe in show cage training. This outstanding Light Green cock enjoys a few moments of solitude in an old show cage attached to its stock cage.

Chris and Arthur Snell:

We believe that our show preparation as described in chapter 2 is one of the main reasons for our success. Spraying with plain cold water, a good diet and plenty of exercise when moulting all play their part. Budgerigars need to grow and develop their muscles. Plenty of training and not too much showing is also a rule to follow. Never forget that a good, clean show cage makes all the difference on the show bench. A typical show team of Light Greens, for us, is four adult cocks, two adult hens, four breeder cocks and four breeder hens. When there are separate class for Dark Greens we like to show a couple of these and at the BS Club Show we enter a team of six Light Green cocks.

Jorge De Pina:

If you win with a Budgerigar that is not fit or has not been properly prepared you are lucky. You should not expect to win if your bird is not in condition so you must always do everything in your power to prepare them properly; no pin feathers (you can get rid of these), well-trimmed masks and well trained. In the UK a top quality show cage can help a bird but, in Brazil, they are provided at the show. They are all the same but not as good as in the UK. I like to enter eight or 10 Light Greens in a class to make a big impact. Also, it is not unknown for a judge to "miss" a good Budgerigar. I like the so-called American system which we use in Brazil. The top prize winners are selected from the top 10 any age cocks, the top 10 any age hens, the top 10 young cocks and the top 10 young hens. This system works well for me. It is unfair for a super Budgerigar to be ignored for the rest of a show just because it came second in its class to the best Budgerigar in show. My Greens are so strong that I regularly get six of them in a top 10 line-up. Show cage training is important because a Budgerigar will not win unless it is on the perch. Budgerigars that look happy in a show cage stand much more chance than those that look frightened. Having said all that, I am sorry to say that some judges never seem to look further than a Budgerigar's head and mask. A Budgerigar without a big head and a wide face does not stand much chance at a big show.

John Woods:

To show off a Budgerigar to best advantage it must be displayed in a show cage which is not only spotlessly clean but also in good repair, with no chipped paintwork. The Budgerigar itself should have been brought up to its maximum visual potential by regular spraying and tidying up of its mask. Then there is condition. A Budgerigar that is in the peak of condition should be bouncing with vitality. This being the case it should catch the judge's eye. If the bird has quality, everything is in place for it go on and become a winner. No matter how good a Budgerigar may be, if it is just put into a show cage without having been properly prepared, it might not even get into the first seven. Such is the competitiveness at the big Budgerigar shows today. Whenever possible I enter at least two Budgerigars in the same class. One reason for doing this is that if one of them becomes unsettled during the judging process, the other will usually perform well and keep your chances alive. Another reason is that different judges look for slightly different features and so the first of my entries could win under one judge while the second might be preferred by another judge.

How do you go about judging Greens?

Jim Moffat:

In judging Light Greens first impressions are very important. In some respects they are simpler to judge than Opalines, Spangles and Pieds whose markings assume a much greater importance. There is less to go wrong with a Light Green's markings - though that is not to say that some are better marked than others. I first find the bird I like best - the leader - and thereafter it is a question of working back from that by assessing the faults and to what degree they are displayed. Lack of condition, head flecking, lack of spots and a drooping tail all need to be penalised. As far as I am concerned, colour only comes into my consideration (other than an exhibit with a serious colour fault which I have yet to encounter while judging) when two exhibits are closely matched. As I now show at only the BS Club Show or Budgerigar World show I am always exhibiting under specialist judges, but I do not feel strongly on the subject. Budgerigar judges, like football referees, are asked for their opinion and the opinion they give is usually very fair. If you want to assess a judge's ability, watch him buying a Budgerigar. That is the acid test. It is surprising that some well-known names not only have difficulty in deciding which bird to buy but, when they do make their minds up, go on to purchase the wrong one! The Budgerigar Society's colour standard and points allocation for Light Greens has evolved over a long period of years and seems to have stood the test of time very well.

Chris and Arthur Snell:

We are always delighted when invited to judge Greens and both approach the task in the same way. When the class is large - say 40, such as you are likely to encounter at the BS Club Show – we examine every exhibit with the BS standard in mind and reject any that obviously lack quality or are out of condition. We dislike poor deportment, flecking and short masks. This could bring the number down to 20. We then look for the potential winner and set it at the left and continue until the number is reduced to 10. It is then that features such as broken feathers, head flecking, whether both tail feathers are in place, whether there are any extra spots under the cheek patches come into our consideration. We continue by considering finer and finer points. Obviously, good colour is very important. We respect other judges and have no qualms about exhibiting our Greens under judges who do not specialise in the variety. The Budgerigar Society standard for Light Greens is satisfactory, but some judges do not interpret it very well. For example, there are judges who put too much emphasis on minor features such as spots. It is very difficult to define what background is needed to produce a good judge. People who have good Budgerigars – and so spend time looking at them while at home – have a good chance of making good judges and breeders who keep low-quality stock are liable to be poor judges, although it is not always the case. In the final analysis temperament also plays a part. Some judges have it, some do not. As far as show organisation is concerned, at big shows we believe that every judge should have the opportunity of offering an opinion when it comes to choosing best in show.

Jorge De Pina:

I have judged all over South America and at several big shows in the UK. My method is always the same. I sort the exhibits into three categories; good, doubtful and poor quality – and hope that there are enough in the first category to fill the first seven places. If not I have to include the "doubtfuls" but always hope that I need not go any lower than that. I look for the best and put it at the left hand end of the judging stand. Cocks need to look strong and powerful, not fragile, and hens need broad shoulders and capping over their eyes. Hens are very different from cocks. I check for the faults I listed earlier. I particularly hate opalistic markings on Normals and believe it is a fault which should receive the same attention from the administrators as flecking. The BS colour standards are the envy of the world and if they are modified it should only be slightly. Whether a judge keeps Greens or not is beside the point – as long as he appreciates a good Budgerigar. A good judge must be able to judge all of the varieties. It is all about knowing Budgerigars and being confident. One of these qualities is no good without the other. I remember, at an important show, seeing a very experienced, senior judge explaining the importance of condition to a trainee. He became so obsessed with condition that he finished up giving first place to a very fit, small cock that would not have been placed in the first seven by most of the other judges present. I believe he was overcome by the occasion. A top breeder does not necessarily make a good judge.

John Woods:

When judging a large class of Light Greens I first cast my eye along them and move the better exhibits to one side and those which do not have any obvious quality to the other. The rest are placed in the middle. Quite often there is an obvious winner and this is moved into pole position and I start to sort out the placings below this. I then check the birds that I rejected in the first instance to make sure that I have not missed a good one that was not showing itself during the initial appraisal. Up to this point my first impressions are usually correct but then I have to look for the finer points that mean a Budgerigar will be penalised to some degree. These faults, such as a missing tail feather or a couple of broken wing flights detract from the enjoyment of judging because they sometimes result in the best physical specimen being beaten by a lesser individual. Up until now it has been the quality of the exhibits as Budgerigars, rather than as Light Greens, that I have been assessing. Colour and markings are factors that make a difference only when two exhibits are very close together and some measure is needed to separate them – unless they are very serious faults. Head flecking, like any other fault, is penalised according to its degree. There are judges who try to make a name for themselves as judges of a particular variety or colour. In my opinion, a judge should be competent to judge any variety.

How do you see the future of Greens?

Jim Moffat:

There are specialist varieties which now command a large following. As far as I am concerned, they will only challenge the Light Green as the leader of the Budgerigar world when they are as thrilling and stunning as Light Greens. Light Greens will always be one of the most popular varieties and I hope I will be around long enough to breed a few more that will give me, and others, much pleasure.

Chris and Arthur Snell:

Light Greens are stronger now than they have been for a few years. Take the BS Club Show as an example; the Light Green classes are consistently better than those for Grey Greens. Light Greens will go from strength to strength. They are the originals, the best of all colours, and the more people who breed them the better, though we would not wish to see them become the subject of a specialist club. There are too many clubs already and Light Greens will always stand at the head of the mainstream.

Jorge De Pina:

I would like to see more breeders working with Normal Greens: it would make the variety much stronger. I fear this will not happen because not many fanciers seem to have the endurance to set up an excellent stud of one variety. In many studs we see the odd good Green but there is no great quality in depth.

John Woods:

Because Light Greens were virtually the only exhibition variety in the early days, it would be impossible for it ever to return to its former prominence. Even so, the fact that Light Greens are taking top awards at events like the BS Club Show is good news for the variety. It is not only a testament to their quality, success also generates interest in any variety. Size is the biggest problem facing the people responsible for setting exhibition standards. The present Budgerigar Society figure of 8½in (21.6cm) is not very realistic. A length of 9½in (24.1cm) would be much nearer the mark for today's Budgerigars. Any larger than that would be storing up problems of lost fertility and style. If anyone wants a bird bigger than that they can always move to keeping Parrakeets.

CHAPTER 7

COLOUR EXPECTATIONS

The subject of Budgerigar colour expectations could fill a book on its own – in fact it HAS filled a book and anyone who wants to delve deeper into the subject should read Taylor and Warner's *Genetics for Budgerigar Breeders*.

Understanding genetics CAN help when it comes to breeding good Budgerigars – particularly when recessive varieties are involved – but it must be stressed that many of the breeders who have bred the best Budgerigars in the world have had only a sketchy knowledge of the subject. So, if you find the subject difficult to understand you will be in good company, and should not worry unduly. For the benefit of those who are interested, and to assist understanding of some of the pairings recommended by the experts, there follow a few examples of how colour expectations can be calculated.

The first fact that needs to be understood is that, in every case, there are TWO factors controlling every individual colour and variety. In this book, the letters used to denote these are not necessarily the ones that are used in serious text books, but have been chosen to make it easier for the inexperienced to understand. So Green is represented by the letter "G" and Blue by "B". When it comes to looking at Dark factor Budgerigars, "L" will represent a light factor and "D" will stand for a dark factor. As explained earlier, each colour series comes in three levels of darkness; Light, Medium and Dark. In the Green series these equate with Light Green, Dark Green and Olive, while in the Blue series they equal Skyblue, Cobalt and Mauve. Like colour, darkness is controlled by TWO factors. To make it simple, let us say a Light has two light factors ("LL"), a Dark has two dark factors ("DD") and a Medium has one light factor and one dark ("LD"). When two Budgerigars mate, each gives ONE of its colour factors to each chick. The possible combinations can be represented by a grid of four squares.

So what happens when two Medium Budgerigars mate and each parent passes on one of its factors to each chick?

		Medium	
		L	D
Medium	L	LL	LD
	D	LD	DD

A quarter of the chicks will be "LL" (Light), a half will be "LD" (Medium) and a quarter will be "DD" (Dark). Translated into colours, this means that two Dark Greens paired together will produce Light Greens, Dark Greens and Olives.

Now let us look at the relationship between a dominant (Green) and a recessive (Blue). A Green Budgerigar's two colour letters are both "G"s. So a Green is "GG". In the same way "BB" indicates a Blue. The next grid shows what happens when a Green mates with a Blue.

		Green	
		G	G
Blue	B	GB	GB
	B	GB	GB

All of the combinations - hence all of the chicks - are the same, "GB" which describes a Budgerigar that looks like a Green but can produce Blues. It is called a Green split Blue (usually written Green/Blue). Let us take it one step further and see what happens when two Green split Blues are mated together.

		Green split Blue	
		G	B
Green split Blue	G	GG	GB
	B	GB	BB

A quarter of the chicks will be "GG" (Greens), a half will be "GB" (Green split Blue, like their parents) and a quarter will be "BB" - Blues! That is how Blue Budgerigars can be bred from two that look just like Greens.

By combining the results of the grids it is possible to include combinations of Light Green, Dark Green, Olive, Skyblue, Cobalt and Mauve into your calculations. However, there is a complication when you come to Dark Green/Blue in that the colours they produce are influenced by whether the Dark factor has been inherited with the Green component of the bird or the Blue. Typically, a Dark Greens/Blue Type I has its Dark factor connected with Green and, as a consequence, tends to produce more Dark

Greens/Blue and Skyblues when paired with a Skyblue. A Dark Green/Blue Type II has its dark factor connected with Blue and, when paired with a Skyblue, tends to produce more Light Greens/Blue and Cobalts.

The above description of the dominance of Greens over Blues can be carried straight over to explain the relationship between Grey Greens and Greens but, in this case, it is the Grey Green which is dominant and the Green is recessive. To be strictly accurate, a Grey Green is a Green with a Grey factor added but to simplify the following calculation it will be considered as a factor in its own right and allocated the letter "R". So a double-factor Grey Green (DF) will be designated "RR" and a single-factor Grey Green (SF) will be represented by "RB" (one Grey Green factor and one Green factor).

The following grid demonstrates what happens when a Grey Green (DF) is paired with a Green:

		Grey Green (DF)	
		R	R
Green	B	RB	RB
	B	RB	RB

All the chicks will be "RB" (single-factor Grey Greens), looking like Grey Greens but capable of producing Greens if paired appropriately.

Many newcomers to the Fancy are surprised when a Green appears in the nest of two Grey Greens. Following the example of the grid which showed two Greens/Blue being paired together to show what happens when two single-factor Grey Greens are paired together. They will produce double-factor Grey Greens, single-factor Grey Greens and Greens. Try it!

For those who have no wish to calculate colour expectations, the following tables will prove useful.

TABLE 1: Pairings involving Light Greens, Dark Greens and Olives.

Pairing*	Expectations (cocks and hens)
Light Green × Light Green	Light Green
Light Green × Dark Green	Light Green Dark Green
Light Green × Olive	Dark Green
Dark Green × Dark Green	Light Green Dark Green Olive
Dark Green × Olive	Dark Green Olive
Olive × Olive	Olive

* *(It makes no difference which colour is the cock and which is the hen)*

TABLE 2: Pairings involving Greens and Blues

Pairing*	Expectations (cocks and hens)
Green × Green	Green
Green × Blue	Green/Blue
Green × Green/Blue	Green Green/Blue
Green/Blue × Green/Blue	Green Green/Blue Blue
Green/Blue × Blue	Green/Blue Blue
Blue × Blue	Blue

* *(It makes no difference which colour is the cock and which is the hen)*

TABLE 3: Pairings involving Grey Greens and Greens

Pairing*	Expectations (cocks and hens)
Green × Green	Green
Green × Grey Green (DF)	Grey Green (SF)
Green × Grey Green (SF)	Grey Green (SF) Green
Grey Green (SF) × Grey Green (SF)	Grey Green (DF) Grey Green (SF) Green
Grey Green (SF) × Grey Green (DF)	Grey Green (DF) Grey Green (SF)
Grey Green (DF) × Grey Green (DF)	Grey Green (DF)

* *(It makes no difference which colour is the cock and which is the hen)*

Further copies of this book and details about others in the "All about..." series can be obtained from:

F. Wright,
31 Redford Avenue,
Wallington,
Surrey, SM6 9DT.

Tel: 081-647 6378

Ask for details of quantity and club discounts

The next books in the "All about . . " series are to be published in 1993. They will be:

All about Blues,
All about Greys and Grey Greens,
All about Spangles.

"The Budgerigar Man" The Harry Bryan way of breeding successful exhibition Budgerigars is still available from F. Wright at the above address. Price £9.95 plus £2 post and packing (£3 overseas).